D1257375

Power and
discontent

WILLIAM A. GAMSON

Professor of Sociology and Research Sociologist
Center for Research on Conflict Resolution
The University of Michigan
Ann Arbor, Michigan

WITHDRAWN FROM UNIVERSITY OF PENNSYLVANIA LIBRARIES

1968

THE DORSEY PRESS

Homewood, Illinois

© William A. Gamson 1968

All rights reserved. No part of this publication may be reproduced, stored in a retrieval system, or transmitted, in any form or by any means, electronic, mechanical, photocopying, recording, or otherwise, without the prior written permission of the copyrightholder.

First Printing, March, 1968

HM
136
G34 cop. 2

Library of Congress Catalog Card No. 68-17044

Printed in the United States of America

UNIVERSITY
of
PENNSYLVANIA
LIBRARIES

TO BLANCHE AND EDWARD GAMSON

Vg-15 39355.2 — Dup. Id.

D., W. U.

Preface

This book began with a desire to make sense of the intense feelings and actions generated by certain issues, particularly fluoridation, in a series of small New England communities. As I wrestled with these microcosms, similar stirrings were taking place in the nation as a whole. I began to hear echoes of the community conflicts I observed in the protests of the civil rights movement and student activists, in the triumphant cries of Goldwater enthusiasts at the Republican convention of 1964, and in the anguished words of urban Negroes in the aftermath of riots. What began as the theoretical introduction to a research monograph increasingly took on a life of its own. Community conflict retreated from center stage and the research I had originally intended to describe was reported elsewhere in separate articles. Gradually the genre changed from the carefully limited explanation of well-defined phenomena to a discursive essay, with fluid boundaries, on a topic of endless complexity.

The themes of this essay have often been treated by others and treated with imagination and eclat. I doubt that I would have had the temerity to tread this well-worked territory if I had not more or less wandered into it without premeditation. As it is, I found closure forced moré by the discipline of writing than by the topic or my state of thinking about it. Loose ends and undeveloped points remain and I would have included some phrase in the title indicating a tentative state of thought if this were not such an obvious form of special pleading.

So much has been written about power and discontent that I could hardly hope to discharge my intellectual debts even if I were aware of them all. Let me mention a few of which I am particularly conscious, since this serves both to acknowledge the stimulation they have given me and to borrow luster for this book from the company it keeps. They include E. E. Schattschneider's *The Semi-Sovereign People*, Ralf Dahrendorf's *Class and Class Conflict in Industrial Society*, Neil J. Smelser's *Theory of Collective Behavior*, David Easton's *A Systems Analysis of Political Life*, Harold D. Lasswell and Abraham Kaplan's *Power and Society*, and a number of works by Robert A. Dahl and Talcott Parsons.

Many of the ideas in this book stem from a long series of seminars with Donald Blain and Richard Taub. In retrospect, these meetings seem particularly exciting and valuable. They were characterized by intellectual playfulness and vigorous debate without ego defensiveness. Stephen Berger later joined these meetings and participated in the same spirit. There were also a good many students in my political sociology seminar whose original ideas and critical reactions to my arguments have contributed a great deal to the evolution of this book. At the risk of slighting many, I will specifically acknowledge some: Paul Potter, Thomas Hayden, Rosabeth Kanter, Andy Michener, Zeke Hasenfeld, Samuel Friedman, James McEvoy, Alan Guskin, and Jeffery Paige.

I am grateful to Guy E. Swanson for his critical comments and encouragement on an earlier draft of this book. Dorsey consultants Robin Williams and Everett K. Wilson also made many helpful suggestions for revision. The Center for Research on Conflict Resolution gave me needed facilities and support and a glittering set of colleagues with similar intellectual interests. Finally, my wife's trenchant criticisms of an earlier draft led me to rework large portions of this book. I remember my annoyance at the time as she forced me to face openly a number of issues which I had slurred. Now that I have done the additional work required, my annoyance has given way to gratitude that she resisted my obvious desire to have done with this project when it was still only half-baked.

Martha's Vineyard   W. A. G.
July, 1967

Table of contents

1

Introduction

There are not many words so evocative as "power." In the hands of the worthy, it is the motor which propels us to the promised land. If we had it, we could correct injustices and find exciting new ways of achieving our goals. In the hands of the unworthy, we can be grateful when it is only frittered away on personal profit; it might have been used for malevolent social purposes. Because power evokes potential without direction, we can be simultaneously excited by its possibilities for creation and alarmed by its possibilities for injury.

Social scientists, presumably, are not immune to such emotions about the word and the phenomena that it describes. It is not surprising, therefore, that some of them have tamed the power theme. It has become harnessed, its wildness curbed by a perspective which removes its threatening aspects. Power as an instrument for the achievement of personal goals becomes muted, a theme secondary to the use of power to achieve collective goals.

But if power has been domesticated for some, there are others for whom the threatening aspects remain central, typically through an emphasis on the pervasiveness of conflict. This book is not intended as a polemic to correct a "misguided" emphasis in sociology. The tamer view of power has provided and continues to provide a large number of insights, many of them extremely subtle. If it leads to the neglect of certain questions, there has been no shortage of sociologists and political scientists who continue to address themselves to the clash of competing interest groups, the mobilization of political support and the like.

Both perspectives on power are important but their relation to each other is frequently problematic. They appear to address the same questions when they are frequently asking complementary questions. They may, it will be argued here, be viewed as dual perspectives on the same relationship and process. Each perspective represents a different vantage point with a set of questions appropriate to a group in that position. If we want to understand the process, we must take both perspectives and clearly recognize when we are in one or the other stance.

TWO PERSPECTIVES ON POWER AND DISCONTENT

Eventually I shall argue that both the benign and the threatening emphases among students of power concern a single relationship between *authorities* and *potential partisans.* One view takes the vantage point of potential partisans and emphasizes the process by which such groups attempt to influence the choices of authorities or the structure within which decisions occur. The second view takes the vantage point of authorities and emphasizes the process by which they attempt to achieve collective goals and to maintain legitimacy and compliance with their decisions in a situation in which significant numbers of potential partisans are not being fully satisfied. But before attempting to present this argument, it is necessary to develop each perspective in turn.

The influence perspective

"Who gets what, when, how?", Harold Lasswell (1936) asked more than 30 years ago. Most of the seeds of the influence perspective are buried in this deceptively simple question. It turns our attention to the allocation of things that are highly valued in a society and, more specifically, to the process of allocation. It directs us to the study of political life "by asking what can be understood about the distribution and use of power" (Easton, 1953, p. 106).

Neither Lasswell nor anyone else really tries to answer this question in its full breadth, but it has produced a number of intertwined partial answers. These answers have a number of important things in common which justify viewing them as part of the same general perspective. They are all conflict oriented, describing a process in which regulated or unregulated conflict plays a central role. They start with a system whose actors have competing wants or demands, who cannot by the very nature of things all be simultaneously satisfied. They are concerned with the power of the actors in the system rather than with the system as a whole. They want to know why some actors are successful in getting what they want while others are not. They are concerned with the discontent of actors because of its implications for the mobilization of slack resources, not because of its implications for system integration.

In discussing some of the work on the influence perspective, it is convenient to divide different strands. This is a matter of convenience only, for my intention here is not to make distinctions among them but to view them as united by the kind of common perspective described above.[1]

The interest group strand. Under the influence of Harold Lasswell (1930; 1936) and Arthur Bentley (1908) among others, political scientists broke out of the sterility of treating politics as the study of formal governmental institutions. The alternative they proposed focused on the political process and assumed that "of the vast variety of activity involved in political situations, that of the persons within the governmental and party structure is only a manifest and small part when compared with the importance of non-governmental social groups" (Easton, 1953, p. 172). Thereafter, political scientists became increasingly interested in the operation of social

---

[1]Cf. Dahl (1961), pp. 5-6, for a somewhat parallel discussion of answers to the question, "Who governs?"

class and ethnic ties as a basis of political activities. Interest groups and pressure groups were urged as the primary units of political analysis rather than formal governmental structures.

"Whatever the bases of group interest may be," wrote V. O. Key, Jr. (1952, p. 24), "the study of politics must rest on an analysis of the objectives and composition of the interest groups within a society. . . . The chief vehicles for the expression of group interest are political parties and pressure groups. Through these formal mechanisms groups of people with like interest make themselves felt in the balancing of political forces." The study of politics in this view, becomes the study of influence and conflict among such groups with some attention to the functions of government as a broker and referee. In other words, it is important to study how any government manages and regulates conflict, but the "principal driving forces in politics are class interests and group interests; they make themselves felt regardless of the kind of government or social organization that exists" (Key, 1952, p. 174).

David Truman (1953), writing in a similar vein, devotes a great deal of attention to the strategy and tactics of such groups, centering particularly around the problem of access. The assumption of conflict of interest runs through the discussion. "The activities of political interest groups imply controversy and conflict, the essence of politics" (Truman, 1953, p. 502). Earl Latham (1952, p. 35) is equally explicit on conflict among groups as the basic fact of political life, government being assigned the role of broker. "The legislature referees the group struggle, ratifies the victories of the successful coalitions, and records the terms of the surrenders, compromises, and conquests in the form of statutes."

Center stage in such a perspective is held by the interest groups who attempt influence, not by the authorities who receive it and must respond with some decisions or policies. There is an important problem of collective decision arising from the fact that the groups have different preferences. And furthermore, some have more resources than others, some are able to form winning coalitions, some are more skillful in their exploitation of available resources, and in other ways there is much to be examined as various actors try to influence the distribution of power and the outcome of important policy decisions. Discontent is important because the various competitors coexist in an uneasy and unstable equilibrium; and from time to time, "one class or group becomes discontented with the existing state of things and the processes of politics go into operation to produce a new equilibrium" (Key, 1952, p. 25).

The political party strand. Closely related to the interest group answer to the question of allocation, although critical of it in certain respects, is a literature which emphasizes political party competition for public office as a central fact of political life. Political parties are not, in this view, groups of people united on some common policies which they are organized to pursue. Rather, a "party is a group whose members propose to act in concert in the competitive struggle for political power" (Schumpeter, 1947, p. 283). They furnish themselves, in this realistic (or cynical) view, with an appropriate set of principles, planks, and policies, much as a department store furnishes itself with various products and brands which it hopes will attract customers from its competitors.[2]

Those who emphasize the importance of electoral competition see the American or British type of political party as more than merely a collection of interest groups. The party, in this view, dominates and uses the pressure group rather than the reverse. "The amount of bargaining that [a party has] to do with special-interest groups," argues Schattschneider (1960, p. 54), "is limited by the fact that each party must cope primarily with its *party* opposition. Neither party can afford to make excessive concessions to any pressure group." In American politics, the two parties monopolize elections,

---

[2]Political parties, in this argument, play a role analogous to the business firm in economic theory. Cf. Anthony Downs, *An Economic Theory of Democracy* (New York: Harper & Row, 1957).

"the greatest single channel to power in the whole regime" (p. 57). "If there are twenty thousand pressure groups and two parties, who has the favorable bargaining position?" Schattschneider asks (p. 57).

But in spite of this different emphasis, this answer shares much with the interest group answer. Party organization and party tactics become the focus rather than interest group organization and tactics but the focus on competition for scarce values remains central. To use Schattschneider's aphorism, "The big game is the party game because in the last analysis *there is no political substitute for victory in an election*" (1960, p. 58). It is the influence game which is of concern here—the explanation of why some are more successful than others in the pursuit of their interests, of what the consequences are of various strategies and tactics of influence.

One can, by a slight turn of the screw, ask slightly different questions about party competition—questions which emphasize the conflict regulation or integrative aspects of party competition and examine the two-party *system*. These will be contrasted with the influence perspective in the discussion below, but here we are concerned with political party and electoral competition as an answer to how things that are highly valued in a society get allocated.

The basic conflict group strand. Political party competition is only one axis of conflict and is applicable only in a limited number of societies. There are other axes which may underlie party conflict and be just as applicable in countries which do not have competing political parties. One that has certainly received its share of attention is the ownership or control of property.

For Marx, relation to the means of production is the foundation of a society's social and political institutions, and conflict among groups with different property relations is the major source of large-scale societal change. The antagonism between those without property and those who possess it is fundamental to understanding the organization of society and government. "Since the State is the form in which the individuals of a ruling class assert their common interests, and in which the whole civil society of an epoch is epitomized, it follows that the State acts as an intermediary for all community institutions, and that these institutions receive a political form," wrote Marx in *German Ideology*.[3] Government, in this argument, is not a set of officials acting as agents of a society and attempting to pursue various collective goals, nor is it a broker among a plurality of competing groups. Rather, it is an instrument for maintaining privilege, a vehicle for one major group in a society to maintain an advantageous position in the pursuit of those things that are valued in the society.

Dahrendorf has suggested a useful and important generalization of the Marxian axis of conflict by treating property relations as a special case of authority relations. Drawing on Geiger (1949) and Burnham (1941), Dahrendorf argues that "property is in its sociological aspect . . . a permission to exclude others from control over an object. . . . Wherever there is property there is authority, but not every form of authority implies property. Authority is the more general social relation" (Dahrendorf, 1959, p. 137).

To single out property relations as the only important axis of conflict, he argues, is to give undue emphasis to one aspect of authority. Class conflict remains central for Dahrendorf but class takes on a new and more general meaning than it had for Marx. "Classes are social conflict groups the determinant . . . of which can be found in the participation in or exclusion from the exercise of authority within any imperatively coordinated association" (Dahrendorf, 1959, p. 138). The key to social organization and, especially, social change is the clash between those who have authority and those who do not, although there may be other important sources of conflict as well. Dahrendorf is more ambiguous than Marx on whether those with authority use such a position for the furtherance of private ends or act as agents of the whole society. As I will argue below, he quite properly moves back and forth between

---

[3]Quoted from excerpts included in Bottomore and Rubel (1956, p. 223).

an influence and a social control perspective, but at this point
I wish to emphasize his answer to questions of allocation.
From this perspective, the instruments of authority are most
important scarce resources over which groups with conflicting
goals grapple. Legitimate power is the grand prize because it
makes it possible to reconcile the losers to their disadvantaged
position. Authority is preferable to any other kind of power
because it has a built-in "cooling mechanism,"[4] a device for
allowing those who fail in a power struggle to accept the consequences with good grace.

The conflict group answer addresses the same questions as
the answers discussed above. The existence of actors with different and conflicting interests is taken as a premise. Understanding the relative power of these actors and their means of
competition helps us to understand why some groups in society get more than others. Discontent is important because
it is related to the organization and mobilization of "have-
not" groups and to their ability to produce different outcomes in the arena of conflict.

The elite group strand. There is an ambiguity of perspective in the conflict group strand that becomes even more pro-
nounced in the literature on elites. This ambiguity emerges in
the dual aspects of authority as personal resource and public
resource. Authority may, from one perspective, have its locus
in the social system and be exercised by individuals acting as
agents for the whole. Or, it may be exercised on behalf of
some subgroup which has conflict with other subgroups, the
group with authority being distinguished because it carries
this important weapon in its arsenal of influence. Only the
latter emphasis involves an influence perspective. Many writers
shift back and forth between these views and this presents no
particular problems if we recognize that at particular points
in discussion here, we may be considering only part of an
author's argument and concern.

---

[4]The term "cooling mechanism," a relatively recent addition to the sociologist's patois, comes from Goffman (1964). He explores social system analogues to
the con man's handling of the danger that his mark or victim may squawk.

These observations are particularly pertinent in discussing theorists who talk of the rulers and the ruled. Are the rulers a self-serving subgroup, disinterested servants of society, or some complicated mixture of both? The influence perspective on such an elite does not argue that authorities operate exclusively or even primarily in their own interest but it *is* concerned with the self-interested aspect of how they operate.

This is precisely the line of inquiry Lasswell takes in his classic, *Politics: Who Gets What, When, How* (1936). His answer focuses on how an elite uses its power to acquire the desirable things in a society and the nature of its challenges from counterelites. It is concerned with how certain groups achieve positions of power and what they do to maintain such an advantageous position. C. Wright Mills's analysis of power in American society (1956) asks the same questions in a more specific context.

Classical elite theorists such as Machiavelli, Pareto, and Mosca have all been concerned with what determines the success of an elite. A central part of this success is skill in the struggle with nonelites or counterelites. "Success" here is ambiguous for it need not imply any underlying conflict between rulers and ruled. However, this question is made somewhat irrelevant by treating the struggle for positions of authority as an end in itself. "Every power group seeks to acquire authority or to exercise effective power over authorities," Lasswell and Kaplan argue (1950, p. 137). Without making any assumptions at all about how such authority is used, it is undeniably scarce and highly valued, and to study the struggle for it is to study one important part of the allocation process.

Unifying concerns in the influence perspective. With all the variety and disagreement among the various strands of thought discussed above, the writers mentioned share a common perspective on power and discontent. They are all addressing the same fundamental questions, share certain working assumptions, and collectively may be contrasted with the complementary perspective discussed below. The common

elements, to which I have frequently alluded, may be summarized as follows:

1. The point of orientation is that of actors in the system
rather than the system as a whole. The analysts of influence
do not view things from above or outside of the system but
from the standpoint of participants with wants or demands
that to some degree conflict with those of other participants.
Lasswell and Kaplan make the point quite strongly: "To speak
of society as a whole as a power holder is to miss the whole
point of political analysis. Power is distributive, and the aim
of political science is to determine how and on what basis it
is distributed" (1950, p. 96).

2. The concern is with, to use Schelling's (1960) apt phrase,
the strategy of conflict rather than the regulation of conflict.
The influence theorists are concerned with how groups try to
get what they want and the conditions under which they succeed, rather than with the consequences of such attempts for
the stability or integration of the system. The scope of conflict is important not because it may threaten the system but
because, to quote Schattschneider (1960, p. 4), "every change
in the scope of conflict has a bias; it is partisan in its nature.
. . . We are bound to suppose," he concludes (p. 8) ". . . that
the control of the scale of conflict has always been a prime
instrument of political strategy, whatever the language of politics may have been."

3. Discontent is viewed as an opportunity or a danger for
particular subgroups, not as a problem of social control. It is
important because of its consequences for mobilization of potential influence. Such consequences are possible because of
the existence in most political systems of what Dahl calls
"slack resources" (1961). Discontent can take up the slack
which means that new resources enter the political arena and
may alter the relative power positions of the participants. "If
slack resources provide the political entrepreneur with his
dazzling opportunity," Dahl writes (1961, p. 309) "they are
also the source of his greatest danger. For nearly every citizen
in the community has access to unused political resources. . . ."

The social control perspective

There is another way of looking at power, one which asks
a different but equally valid set of questions. "Politics is often
regarded simply as a struggle over scarce values," argues Mitchell (1962, p. 142). "... To concentrate upon the allocation
of values and the struggles of politics, however, is to have a
one-sided picture of . . . politics." The other side asks about
the collective purposes to which power is put rather than its
private purposes. It is concerned with the power of the system, i.e., the ability of a society to mobilize and generate resources to attain societal goals. If one had to reduce this perspective to a question analogous to the earlier question of who
gets what, when, how, it might be: How does leadership operate to achieve societal goals most efficiently while at the
same time avoiding costly side effects?

There is no intention to belittle the importance of this
question in suggesting, as I did earlier, that it domesticates
the power theme. Conflict remains a central problem but the
social scientist is now above the battle—the third party who
is concerned with conflict regulation and resolution instead
of the partisan concern of how to win. The vantage point of
the system as a whole is a lofty and comfortable one which
allows us to view problems of how the pie is divided with some
detachment while we address the question of enlarging the
pie. But the closeness of a vantage point to the scene of
battle is a neutral fact in itself. Depending on where we stand
we see some things better than others and there is no denying
the fact that the size of the pie is variable and that important
intellectual insights result from stepping back.

The system as power holder. It is a useful working assumption that every social organization is composed of elements with both individual, conflicting interests and with collective interests. The economists' concept of "public goods"
is a useful one for talking about the ability of the system to
achieve collective goals. "A common, collective, or public
good" is defined by Olson (1965, pp. 14-15) "as any good

such that, if any person X_i in a group $X_1, \ldots X_i, \ldots,$ X_n consumes it, it cannot feasibly be withheld from the others in that group. . . . The achievement of any common goal or the satisfaction of any common interest means that a public or collective good has been provided for that group."

One may talk about power as the ability of a system to utilize and mobilize resources for the achievement of collective goods. It is then possible to talk about increases in power without assuming that such an increase implies a corresponding decrease in power for some unit. It is just this perspective that Parsons brings to bear in his brilliant and lucidly written essay on Mills's *The Power Elite* (Parsons, 1960, Ch. 6, "The Distribution of Power in American Society"). Mills adopts one main version of power, Parsons argues: a zero-sum or, more precisely, a constant-sum conception. "The essential point . . . is that, to Mills, power is not a facility for the performance of function . . . on behalf of the society as a system, but it is interpreted exclusively as a facility for getting what one group, the holders of power, wants by preventing another group, the 'outs,' from getting what it wants" (Parsons, 1960, p. 220). Granting that power has a distributive aspect, "it also has to be produced and it has collective as well as distributive functions. It is the capacity to mobilize the resources of the society for the attainment of goals for which a general 'public' commitment has been made, or may be made" (Parsons, 1960, p. 221).

Human ecologists share this emphasis on power as an attribute of a system rather than its subparts. "Every social group or system is an organization of power," Hawley writes (1963, p. 422). "The community, for example, may be conceived as an energy system. That is, as a system of relationships among functionally differentiated units, the community constitutes a mobilization of power—the capacity to produce results—for dealing with the environment, whether physical or social" (Hawley, 1963, p. 423). Power, in this conception, is clearly a property of a system.

Whatever power an individual might appear to possess is in effect attached to the office he occupies in a system. He acquires power by attaining to an office and he loses it when he is separated from the office. But the acquiring and losing of power is illusory; the property belongs rather with the office or, better still, to the system in which the office is a specialized function (Hawley, 1963, p. 423).

The distribution of power is significant in such a perspective because concentration of power increases the ability of the system to produce collective goods. While power concentration is not a sufficient condition for successful collective action, its absence may be sufficient to defeat an action "as a result of power being so diffusely held that mobilization of the community cannot be accomplished" (Hawley, 1963, p. 424).

Clearly, this perspective on power is asking a different set of questions than those addressed by the influence perspective. The concern is not with the distribution of private goods but with the production of collective goods. Where earlier we might ask about the relative advantages or disadvantages of various actors in the system, here we ask about the relative efficiency or effectiveness of different forms of social organization.

The system as conflict regulator.   The social control perspective is not exclusively concerned with the achievement of collective goals. There is a strong interest in conflict as well since a system cannot function effectively if it must devote too much of its resources to problems of integration and conflict management. The ability to handle conflict successfully is a critical leadership skill which can be encumbered or eased by various political and social arrangements. "The crucial problem in politics is the management of conflict," Schattschneider argues (1960, p. 71). "No regime could endure which did not cope with this problem. All politics, all leadership and all organization involves the management of conflict."

One tradition of conflict regulation emphasizes a pluralistic social structure and the presence of multiple, overlapping group memberships. A rich structure of such groups serves to encourage the compromise of demands. The existence of overlap between groups creates a peculiar circumstance: the boundary of one group is a potential line of cleavage in another. A conflict between two overlapping groups cannot be pressed to the fullest by either group without running the risk that it will create a breach within itself. Those who belong to both conflicting groups are natural compromisers and mediators. As Truman (1953, p. 510) puts it, "It is the competing claims of other groups within a given interest group that threaten its cohesion and force it to reconcile its claims with those of other groups active on the political scene." Superimposition of cleavages, on the other hand, makes conflict more intense and difficult to regulate.

In discussing interest groups above, we considered their importance as a vehicle of influence; here we are concerned with a *set* of interest groups and the consequences of their interrelations for the stability of the system. A similar shift in focus takes place in viewing political parties. The political party *system* rather than the political party becomes the central concern in the social control focus. One can then ask what contribution an electoral contest has made to the exacerbation or lessening of cleavages in a society and to what degree the election represents "a process of consent" (Janowitz and Marvick, 1956). Similar questions are asked by Parsons (1959) in discussing a "theoretical model of a two-party system." Here his argument goes beyond treating the electoral process simply as a regulator of conflict; it is also important as a generator of power. In fact, the two-party system emerges as an absolutely ingenious device for producing multiple public goods simultaneously and effectively. There is little concern here with its impact on the distribution of private goods, on the allocation rather than the generation of power.

There is a virtually limitless literature on the question of what holds a society together—all of which could be construed as addressing the problem of conflict regulation. My construction here is narrower: *it treats conflict regulation as the man-*

agement or control of the use of power by actors in a social system. Such an idea is central to Easton's (1965) treatment of a political system as one which processes demands and produces authoritative decisions. There is inherent conflict built into the fact that every political system can only handle a limited number of demands. If the demands become too heavy it will "undermine the capacity of a system to produce its characteristic outputs, authoritative decisions" (Easton, 1965, p. 57).

It is not uncommon for writers who are concerned with social conflict to change perspectives, speaking at one point from the standpoint of an actor in the system and at another point from the standpoint of the system. Dahrendorf, for example, writes not only on the problem of allocation but on the regulation of conflict as well, suggesting three factors which make it effective.

First, for effective conflict regulation to be possible, both parties to a conflict have to recognize the necessity and reality of the conflict situation and, in this sense, the fundamental justice of the cause of the opponent. . . . A second prerequisite of effective conflict regulation is the organization of interest groups. So long as conflicting forces are diffuse, incoherent aggregates, regulation is virtually impossible. . . . Thirdly, in order for effective regulation to be possible, the opposing parties in social conflicts have to agree on certain formal rules of the game that provide the framework of their relations (Dahrendorf, 1959, pp. 225-26).

The role of government as conflict regulator or broker of competing demands is emphasized in this perspective. But officials also serve as influencers. For Easton (1965), the conflict processors can and do act as initiators of demands themselves. And Schattschneider criticizes the view of government as referee, arguing that "private conflicts are taken into the public arena precisely because someone wants to make certain that the power ratio among the private interests most immediately involved shall not prevail" (1960, p. 38). In making these points, Easton and Schattschneider are taking an influence perspective on government rather than a social control perspective—they are concerned with political authorities as one important actor in the system rather than as the embodiment or agents of that system.

Discontent as a source of instability. Closely related to an emphasis on conflict regulation is a concern with discontent as a source of instability. Smelser's *Theory of Collective Behavior* (1963) combines these concerns and might well have been called, alternatively, *A Theory of Conflict Regulation.* Smelser is concerned with the conditions under which collective action takes a noninstitutionalized form. A well-designed system has ways of handling discontent by alleviating the underlying strain or channeling its political expression in an orderly fashion. Smelser's vantage point is nowhere clearer than in his discussion of a

model for containing value-oriented movements. . . . . It involves four kinds of behavior on the part of authorities: (1) Ruling out uninstitutionalized expression of hostility. . . . (2) Ruling out direct challenges to legitimacy. . . . (3) Opening channels for peaceful agitation for normative change and permitting a patient and thorough hearing for the aggrieved groups. . . . (4) Attempting to reduce the sources of strain that initiated the value-oriented movement (Smelser, 1963, p. 364).

There is no corresponding advice to the would-be leaders of a value-oriented social movement on the best strategy for getting started.

The same perspective on discontent is present in Easton's remarks on "the consequences of channel failure" (1965, p. 122). "Demonstrations, riots, mass rallies, and the like have become important mechanisms for expressing and communicating demands. Blockage of demands in these cases has not served to obliterate them. Its consequence has been to transform what might have been a pacific continuous flow of demands into a spasmodically violent, eruptive one." As for Smelser, acute discontent can become a serious problem for the political system unless it is dealt with properly. Discontent is important because it can lead to actions which diminish the effectiveness of the government in the pursuit of collective goals.

Unifying concerns in the social control perspective. There
are two central themes in this perspective but they are closely
interwoven—a concern with the generation of public power
and with the control of private power. As Easton argues,
" . . . a system approach draws us away from a discussion
of the way in which the political pie is cut up and how it happens to get cut up in one way rather than another. . . . [It
provides us instead with a] theoretical framework that helps
us to understand how the very pie itself comes into existence
and changes in its content or structure" (1965, p. 475). Such
a perspective does not compete with but complements theories of allocation "because they are operating at a different
level of analysis" (1965, p. 476). For purposes of contrast
with the influence perspective, the common elements in the
social control perspective may be summarized as follows:

1. The point of orientation is agents of the system or the
system as a whole rather than actors in the system. Mitchell
(1962, p. 268) is quite self-conscious about the shift from this
orientation, following a discussion of the "ways in which the
American polity mobilizes societal resources to attain societal
goals . . . . Our perspectives of the polity will now change from
that of the system attaining goals to that of the individual
members struggling to realize their own private desires." The
former perspective is a view from outside or above the system.

2. The concern is with the regulation of conflict, not with
its strategy and tactics. The question, "Who succeeds and
why?" yields to the question of how such power struggles
among actors may impair the ability of the system to achieve
collective goals.

3. Discontent is a problem for the system to manage, not
an opportunity for actors to increase their influence. Masses
of apathetic and unmotivated citizens reduce the power of
the system. The commitment of its citizens is a critical element in its capacity for achieving collective goals. This stance
toward discontent and social conflict makes appropriate the
choice of the term "social control perspective" to describe it.

INTEGRATING THE TWO PERSPECTIVES

These two disparate perspectives on power and discontent are concerned with the same relationship although they ask different questions about it. This fact gives them a natural unity—each is a partial view but together they form a whole. On the one hand, the relationship may be described as one of potential influence. The agents of influence *(potential partisans)* are those actors who are affected by the decisions and actions of authorities. The targets of influence *(authorities)* are those agents of the system who make binding decisions. When one asks about this relationship as a potential partisan, he takes what was described above as an influence perspective.

On the other hand, this relationship may be described as one of social control. The agents of control are authorities acting in their capacity as agents of the system. The targets of control are potential partisans whose actions can potentially disrupt the orderly functioning of the system. When one asks about this relationship as an authority, he takes what was described above as a social control perspective.

A complete understanding of the relationship between potential partisans and authorities requires that one examine it from the standpoint of both parties. Furthermore, the insight that some given discussion of power and discontent views it from one or the other incomplete vantage point enables us to see more clearly what it omits. It enables us to detect and correct a bias while recognizing the partial validity which may stem from such an analysis. For those writers who shift back and forth, the idea of a dual perspective helps us to sort their arguments and to recognize their connection as alternative vantage points on a single relationship.

The rest of this book is an attempt to develop and clarify this argument and to suggest some specific hypotheses relating influence and social control variables. There are a number of problems associated with the definition of the parties in this relationship. In Chapter 2, the terms potential partisans and authorities are explored in some detail.

A number of writers, most particularly Parsons (1963; 1964) and Easton (1965), have focused on the kind of generalized support or trust which members of a society invest in a political system or its agents. This interest in the degree and nature of trust helps us to identify an important set of variables for predicting the actions of potential partisans toward authorities. The nature of these actions and the resultant social control responses in turn help us to predict the ebb and flow of discontent. In Chapter 3, the nature of the trust relationship between potential partisans and authorities is explored.

The nature of influence by potential partisans requires an extended discussion if we are to keep our bearings in this swampland of a subject. A number of distinctions concerning the exercise of influence are made in Chapter 4. In Chapter 5, potential influence is considered in an analysis that relies heavily on the concept of resources.

The perspective in Chapter 6 shifts to the viewpoint of authorities and considers the nature of social control and the management of discontent. Chapters 7 and 8 attempt to relate influence, political trust, and social control with a series of hypotheses. Finally, Chapter 9 concludes with a discussion of some implications of the argument for the study of social change.

2

Potential partisans and authorities

Complementary perspectives on power and discontent focus
on a relationship between potential partisans and authorities.
What is meant by these terms? Isn't everyone a *potential* partisan? Don't authorities frequently act as partisans? What does
this do to the boundaries of the relationship? Some of these
questions are not easily answered.

AUTHORITIES — use this for the last part of your paper you must

It is helpful to start with the notion of a decision to be
made, a choice among alternatives. For any decision, there
exists some group or individual whose acceptance or rejection
of an alternative is *binding*. The *authorities* are those who,
for any given social system, make binding decisions in that
system. If authority is decentralized and diffuse, every member of the system may be an authority on at least some set of
decisions although these decisions may vary greatly in importance for the system.

No decision has been made until authorities place their
stamp of approval upon a choice. To say that the choice is
binding implies that it can be implemented without the necessity of any further group reviewing the content of the decision. This is essentially what Easton means by the term
authoritative. "A policy is authoritative when the people to
whom it is intended to apply or who are affected by it

21

consider that they must or ought to obey it" (1953, p. 132).
However, the definition here places greater emphasis on the
ability to enforce such a decision. A decision is binding if
either it is accepted as binding (for whatever reason) *or*, if it
is not accepted, legitimate force can be used to implement the
decision. Effective authority is implied here, not merely formal or legal authority.

When is a decision binding?

The above definition is not without ambiguity and an extended example may help to clarify it further. I have deliberately chosen such an example from a situation in which the
legitimacy of a decision was actively called into question—a
conflict between students and administrators at the University
of Michigan. This particular conflict concerned a ruling, issued
by the Office of the Vice President for Student Affairs, which
made certain distinctions among means of political protest
and, in particular, singled out sit-ins in private offices as a violation of university rules. The challenge to this ruling by students did not question the content of the rule but the manner
in which it was made.[1] It took the particular form of a public
claim by the Student Government Council that, because of
the improper manner of decision, the outcome would not be
considered binding. The interesting question arises, were there
authorities for this decision and, if so, who were they?

The decision was binding whether the students chose to
regard it so or not. It was binding because it could have been
enforced had the university administration chosen to do so,
albeit at what might have been prohibitive cost to the university. By this, I mean that if the rule had been violated the
university administration could have taken punitive action

---

[1]The particular incident in question happened to coincide with two other
issues which added considerable strength to the student protest and won it support from many faculty members. However, these connected issues are irrelevant
for the purpose of this example.

against the students and have had such action carried out. If students were expelled, the appropriate university officials would have prevented them from registering for courses, receiving credit, and in other ways receiving the perquisites of being a student.

The above assertions rely on an empirical assumption which might have proven false. It is possible that an effort to enforce a decision may lead to a collapse of the entire authority system—in this case, a situation in which university officials would refuse to carry out the authoritative requests of other university officials. This is unlikely to have been true in this instance although there may well have been severe costs in terms of lost faculty members and students and bitter enmity among those who remained. It is undoubtedly such potential costs that led to the subsequent announcement by the president of the university that the implementation of the rule would be delayed pending clarification by a tripartite committee of students, faculty, and administrators.

The point of this example is that the *capacity* to enforce a decision makes it binding. This capacity may exist even though the consequences of enforcement may lead authorities to change the nature of their choices. The change that occurred in the above example was a change of decision as a result of influence, not a change in the effective authorities for a decision. Some changes do involve a shift in effective authority and the discussion below tries to distinguish such a situation from a number of others in which the effective authorities remain the same.

When does a change in authority occur?

Consider four situations: (1) a reassertion of authority by a group with formal authority that has not been exercising it; (2) a change in the content of a decision in response to the imposition of irresistible force; (3) a change in the people who are filling authority roles with a corresponding decision reversal; and (4) the performance of reviewing or overseeing functions. Only the first of these represents a change in the effective authorities for a decision.

√ 1. *Reclaiming of authority.* Authority is typically delegated and under nonconflict conditions, a body without formal authority may be the effective authority for a decision. If the U.S. Senate Judiciary Committee, for example, recommends private immigration bills that are passed by unanimous consent without independent review by the whole Senate, then the Judiciary Committee rather than the Senate is the effective authority for such decisions.

However, conflict may be both a source and a consequence of the reassertion of effective authority by groups with formal authority. In the university example cited above, the regents of the university would, in less-troubled times, leave the effective authority for rules governing student conduct in the hands of the president. He in turn might leave it with the vice president for student affairs who might delegate it even further to various student groups. Under conditions of university-wide conflict, the effective authority reverts to those bodies with formal authority—the office of the president and, if necessary, the board of regents.

A group with formal but not effective authority may find that it is difficult to assert effective authority when it chooses, and that its own decisions will be challenged in spite of their legal status. An effort to make formal authority effective may produce a crisis in which the authority system is directly challenged and tested. Sykes (1958) points to such efforts as a crucial element in the breakdown of the social order of a prison, a breakdown which may result in riots or other forms of insurrection. He argues that the dynamics of such incidents involve an attempt by prison officials to reclaim authority over areas of decision which have, in effect, been delegated to inmates. In doing so, they undermine the "authority" of those inmates who have been exercising it and who, because of their privileged position, have acquired a strong stake in maintaining order. The destruction of their effective authority leaves a vacuum into which more hostile inmates move. These rebellious leaders are able to mobilize active resistance to formal authorities until some uneasy truce occurs.

Whenever formal and effective authority reside in different bodies, which is to say whenever authority is delegated, the question of who exercises it in any specific situation can become delicate. It is not, however, a conceptual problem. Any time a formal authority chooses to exercise effective authority, it *is* the effective authority even if its exercise of such authority is challenged. At the University of Michigan, the editors of the student newspaper, the *Michigan Daily,* are appointed annually by a Board in Control of Student Publications on the recommendations of the retiring senior editors. However, these recommendations have tended to become automatically accepted and an attempt by the board to reject a recommendation by the senior editors led to a sharp confrontation between the two groups. Despite the board's difficulties, it was the effective authority once it chose to assert itself in this manner, and notwithstanding the fact that the board came off second best in the confrontation. The *Daily* editors were able to mobilize influential allies and to hold out the threat of a strike and thus sway enough members of the board to bring about a reversal. But this is a case of influence, and effective authority is characterized by the absence of the necessity for influence. It is not true that the Board in Control of Student Publications was *unable* to enforce its decision to reject the senior editors' recommendations; it *chose* not to maintain that decision because of its judgment about the consequences of that choice.

There is one exception to the rule that the formal authorities are the effective authorities whenever they choose to be regardless of the conflict generated by this assertion of authority. This exception involves a revolutionary situation. If a group within a society defies the regime, and that regime orders its soldiers to arrest the rebellious group and they are unable to do so, the regime is not exercising effective authority over such a group. The legitimacy of the regime is not the

only issue here although it is involved. The existing authorities may have usurped it, and be loathed by most citizens but
they are the effective authorities if they are able to make
binding decisions. However, their ability to make their decisions binding is very much related to legitimacy since if
their soldiers desert and will not accept their orders, they
lack the capacity to enforce them (unless, as in the case of
South Vietnam, a regime with little or no legitimacy is able
to use another country's soldiers to enforce such decisions).
Who is the effective authority in a system in which groups are
battling over who exercises authority? When this occurs, it
may be treated as two systems. If a "rebel" force is able to
impose and collect taxes in an area in which the "government"
is unable to do this, it is, in effect, the government for that
area in which it is able to exercise effective authority. Ultimately then, who has effective authority must be answered
empirically. In situations in which high legitimacy attaches to
authority one can safely assume that effective authority cor-
responds to formal authority when those who possess it
choose to exercise it; in situations of low legitimacy, one may
not know who exercises effective authority until it is tested.

2. *A forced reversal of a decision.* A situation in which
authorities are "forced" to change an earlier decision under
irresistible pressure does not represent a shift in authorities.
Their earlier decision was binding had they chosen to pay the
personal consequences of enforcing it and the later decision
is equally binding. To say that a decision is binding is not to
say it is irrevocable or that the authorities are independent of
influence. They may even be mere puppets in the hands of
secret groups who manipulate them at will. As Easton points
out (1965, p. 349), "Politically powerful members may well
play the tune to which the authorities dance and in this sense
they effectively dominate the outputs. But without processing
their own demands through the authorities, their demands
would not be converted into recognized systemic outputs."

3. *A change in personnel.* A change in the people who fill
authority roles does not change the binding nature of the

decision. Imagine that, in the midst of a conflict between students and administrators, the board of regents found the president of the university insufficiently malleable and decided to replace him with a man more susceptible to their influence. This new man might well reverse decisions of the earlier president. Does this mean that the first man was not the effective authority for the decision since he was unable to enforce his decision?

The binding character of the decision is attached to the position, not to the individuals who occupy it. The authority stems from the system and is invested in the office. It is the office which possesses the capacity to enforce decisions. To the extent that one goes beyond his office to use personal resources to accomplish his ends, he is exercising influence or leadership rather than authority. This distinction lies at the heart of Richard Neustadt's discussion of *Presidential Power* (1962). " 'Powers' are no guarantee of power. . . . Despite [the President's formal] 'powers' he does not obtain results by giving orders—or not, at any rate, merely by giving orders" (Neustadt, 1962, p. 10). The "powers" of the office of the presidency, not the "power" of the President is covered by the term "authorities."

4. *Performance of an overseeing function.* There may be many situations in which the decisions of one group are subject to subsequent review by another group. Whether the first group is in fact the effective authority for a given decision depends on the necessity of influence. If influence is necessary to get the approval of the other group, the first group is not the effective authority; if influence is unnecessary, the first group is the effective authority.

Any reviewing body is likely to raise certain questions and maintain the right to overrule decisions of the subordinate group if it is not satisfied. Isn't influence always necessary, even if the review is perfunctory and merely pro forma? Even in such situations, it would appear that the manner of presentation is important in keeping the proceeding perfunctory. This ambiguity over the delegation of authority is not simply conceptual—it is an organizational property which is frequently the source of conflict. However, the conceptual ambiguity may be partly handled and a more realistic definition of effective authority maintained by defining a particular kind of review procedure as *not* involving influence. This procedure is illustrated in the following example.

Imagine an organization in which a board of trustees has formal authority to approve or disapprove all major appointees in the organization. However, in normal practice, their review never considers the merits or demerits of recommendations from the chief executive, but simply considers *procedural regularity*. In fact, no questions at all are raised as long as there is no visible controversy. If there is controversy, the board of trustees confines itself to determining if certain specified procedures have been followed: they ask only if the chief executive is functioning in his capacity as agent of the larger collectivity in observing its norms governing the manner of decision. An individual or group can be considered the effective authority for a decision if it is only necessary for it to demonstrate procedural regularity to have its decisions ratified by formal authorities. However, under conditions of severe conflict, procedural regularity may not be sufficient and a group which has usually been the effective authority for a decision may discover it must use influence. In such a situation, a shift in effective authority has occurred and it is no longer making binding decisions.

Authorities as partisans

The discussion above has emphasized that if a group must exercise influence over a decision, it is not the effective authority for that decision. This does not imply that those who occupy authoritative positions never function as partisans on decisions over which they exercise authority. They do, of course, and frequently their authority is itself an important resource used to influence others with authority. Two members of a legislative body may trade votes, each offering his choice on a decision that he is indifferent to for a second vote on a decision that is important to him. When he is using his vote as a resource to influence another, he is not functioning in his role as authority, but he is when he accepts influence. When acting as an agent of influence, his position as an authority is adventitious.

There is no imputation intended that something is wrong with people in authority acting as agents of influence. This is what we usually mean by leadership. "The search for personal influence is at the center of the job of being President," Neustadt writes (1962, p. viii) in his analysis of how a man occupying the office of President of the United States operates to make those powers work for him. If we approve of the outcomes sought by the person in authority, we call it leadership; if we don't approve, we call it "abuse of authority." Put another way, we call it leadership when influence is used in the pursuit of collective interests and misuse of authority when it is used in the interests of some subgroup or individual. Since we are all adept at convincing ourselves that what we want is in the public interest, these two ways of putting it sometimes amount to the same thing.

In any event, it is usually considered quite proper for an individual with authority to act as an advocate on decisions as long as he stays within certain bounds and advocates the "right" thing. In his attempts to influence his colleagues who share authority for a particular decision, he is functioning in the role of partisan rather than authority; later, when it is time for him to vote, he resumes the authority role. Easton wrestles with this same boundary problem in discussing demands which are not "put into" the political system from "the experiences of persons who have acted in roles outside the political sector of society" but have "emerged directly out of political roles themselves" (1965, p. 55). He proposes the term "within-puts" to describe demands generated by those acting in political roles. The solution proposed here is to define the authority role more narrowly and to treat the demands of those with authority as part of a different role.

But to do this does not deny that those who occupy authority roles are important producers of influence attempts as well as producers of binding decisions.

Is it possible to maintain a distinction between a person performing the functions of authority and the functions of influencer when they are such intimately related parts of the same position? After all, a large number of decisions are made in the following fashion: A group of men sit around a table dealing with a number of items on an agenda. They are essentially disinterested in the various matters they are disposing of and are trying conscientiously to make decisions which are best for the collectivity. On most of the matters they discuss, there are no active partisans. People raise questions or issues which they feel need to be considered but no one takes a strong advocacy position. When everyone who has spoken seems reasonably satisfied that a particular decision or policy is sufficient to meet the problem, the group moves on to the next agenda item. Are the participants functioning solely in the role of authorities? If not, at what point are they performing some function other than that of making decisions?

Influence need not involve the traditional model of organized interest groups bringing pressure to bear on authorities. If the group of decision makers in the example above is part of a system of any degree of complexity, then the individuals on the committee are likely to be associated with different parts of the system. Committees are frequently composed with an effort to have all major subdivisions of an organization represented. The items on the agenda will normally be initiated by some subdivision or at least will deal with a problem of special concern to one or more subgroups. Perhaps the sales manager has died and one of the members of the sales staff is now to be promoted to this position. The head of the research division who is a member of the committee making the decision is interested in getting an able man for the job but he is unaffected by the choice except insomuch as the whole organization is affected. He does not know the respective qualifications of the individual staff members. Other

members of the committee may be more immediately involved in the outcome and for this reason, they may be given
the responsibility for presenting the qualifications of various
individuals to the others. They may argue that of 30 eligible
candidates only 2 should be considered prime candidates by
reason of their previous record and seniority. They may have
eliminated a very able junior man for fear that his selection
would be regarded as so insulting by the two senior men that
their loyalty and value to the company would be severely impaired. Between the two senior men, they are uncertain. However, in the course of presenting their relative merits to the
committee they manage to convince themselves and the others that on balance one of the two candidates is the stronger
choice.

It does not seem farfetched to identify and differentiate
these actions between authority and partisan roles. In selecting two from among all the possible candidates for presentation to the committee, the presenters are functioning as authorities, influenced by their conversations with the sales staff
and their anticipation of possible actions from that group of
potential partisans. In presenting the two candidates to the
committee for final choice, they are in a partisan role even
though their own preference is not clear at the moment. The
others will raise questions that may help them to decide their
own preference which, once decided, is likely to be accepted.
For these others, it is a case of "If you are satisfied that X is
the best man, then I'm satisfied too." The essential point here
is that during the influence and discussion process, the authority role is being filled by those who are unaffected by the
choice except insomuch as it affects everybody.

The problem of multiple authorities

One final point on the definition of authorities needs clarification. How does one handle decisions in which several
different bodies independently review an alternative before it
becomes binding? Do the U.S. Senate, the House of Repre-

sentatives, and the President together comprise the authorities
for a proposed federal law? Theoretically, the answer is yes,
for their choices together are both necessary and sufficient to
make it binding. For operational purposes, however, it is useful to adopt a harmless convention. This convention consists
of treating the decisions of separate bodies as separate decisions. Thus, the Senate decides whether to adopt Senate
Bill 999 while the House of Representatives decides whether
to adopt the similar House Bill 777. The Senate-House Con-
ference must decide on how to reconcile the differences and
the President must decide on whether to sign or veto the re-
sulting bill. Each of these, and numerous other decisions (for
example, the decision to give the bill a rule in the house, the
decision to report it out of committee, and so forth) may all
be considered part of a chain of related decisions, each having
its own relevant authorities. By this convention, a body whose
ratification is necessary but not sufficient to make some larger
decision binding is treated as the authorities for a more limited decision.

POTENTIAL PARTISANS

The definition of potential partisans is less problematic
than the definition of authorities but there are still some
ambiguities. Potential partisans may be defined as that set of
actors who, for a given decision, are affected by the outcome
in some "significant" way. They need not perceive the significance of the decision for themselves or have either the inclination or the ability to influence the outcome if they do perceive it.

It will make some difference in the lives of these potential
partisans if one thing rather than another is decided. This is
potentially true of all the authorities involved in any decision.
Any matter, regardless of its intrinsic interest to an authority,
becomes important to him if major rewards and punishments
are made contingent on his choice. In this sense, authorities
confronted with a decision are always a subset of potential

partisans. Because they make binding choices that are important to others, others can *make* the outcomes affect the authorities through the medium of influence.

However, it is worth distinguishing between two meanings of "potential." There are those actors who will be hurt or helped directly by the policies being decided. The word potential applied to them is intended to leave open the question of whether they will attempt influence. There is a double potentiality involved when we apply the term to those who are not directly concerned but who might become concerned via the medium of threats and promises. Such people have the potential for becoming concerned and, once such concern has been established, the further potential for attempting influence. The term potential partisan is reserved for single rather than double potentiality. An authority is a potential partisan only when enough influence has occurred to make the outcome affect him in some significant way. The mere possibility of this occurring is insufficient to make him qualify.

The definition of potential partisan employs a threshold concept in the phrase "affected in some *significant* way." Those above this threshold are not uniformly affected, of course. The magnitude of the effect is an important variable for predicting the probability of influence by different potential partisans. Other variables include their attitudes toward authorities and the political system, their expectations about the likely actions of authorities, and the extent of their political resources. But the question of when potential partisans become actual partisans by attempting influence is a central concern of later chapters and discussion here would be premature.

The organization of potential partisans

Authorities are organized into boards, committees, administrations, legislatures, councils, and so forth; and potential partisans are also more than simply aggregates of unorganized individuals. What are the major units of potential partisans?

Many writers have found it useful to distinguish groups in various degrees of dormancy. Easton, for example, distinguishes organized groups from social groupings. "Individuals fall into such groupings as a result of the possession of certain common social characteristics rather than because of a common effort for the achievement of collective purposes" (1953, p. 186). Such latent groups are "analytically prior to social groups in the sense that the activity and even the interpretation of goals of a formal organization reflect the fundamental social groupings from which its members come" (1953, p. 187). Similarly, Truman (1953) pays a good deal of attention to "potential groups" and the possibility that they may become organized pressure groups.

Dahrendorf (1959) and Ginsberg (1953) use the term "quasi group" in making a similar distinction. Such aggregates of latent interests are a "recruiting field for groups" (Ginsberg, 1953, p. 40). Quasi groups do not have common modes of behavior. "Common modes of behavior are characteristic of *interest groups* recruited from larger quasi-groups . . . and they are the real agents of group conflict" (Dahrendorf, 1959, p. 180).

Later I will want to characterize potential partisan groups by certain general attitudes toward the political system and to do so, it is useful to specify a third degree of organization which lies between the quasi group and the interest group. This third kind of group is not primarily an intermediate stage in the organization and development of an interest group although it may sometimes be this. It is better described as the constituency of an organized interest group. It differs from a quasi group in including some common identification or feeling of political "we," as Lasswell and Kaplan put it (1950, p. 11). Such *solidary groups* are psychological groups in which "egos are emotionally bound together in relation to [political] demands in the name of the identified groups." For such a solidary group to exist, "the persons in the aggregate must take account of the perspectives of the others, identify with the others, be interested in their interests. There is not merely a number of egos making the same demand, for instance, but the demand is made in behalf of a self including the various egos" (1950, p. 30). Interest groups are formal organizations which represent the demands of such solidary groups in the political system.

Solidary groups, then, are neither quasi groups nor interest groups but something in between. They are collections of individuals who think in terms of the effect of political decisions on the aggregate and feel that they are in some way personally affected by what happens to the aggregate. Examples would include ethnic groups such as Jews, Negroes, Italian-Americans, and Irish-Americans; religious groups, some occupational groups, and many other categories depending on the social organizational context. If one were concerned with the U.S. Congress as a system, solidary groups might include "urban congressmen," "Southerners," "farm bloc congressmen" and so forth.

Solidary groups differ in their degree of cohesiveness or solidarity. More specifically, solidarity will be promoted by the following:

1. *Symbolic expressions of the group as a collectivity.* The existence of a name or slogan as a focus for loyalty and identification will enhance solidarity. Formal organizations which are composed predominantly of members of the solidary group help to promote such identification and loyalty. They are a tangible reminder of membership in a collectivity. Furthermore, they may act directly to interpret issues for the members of a solidary group and thus keep salient the idea of a collective interest by speaking in the name of such a group. The American Farm Bureau Federation or the Farmers' Union purports to speak for "farmers" and thus reminds individual farmers that they belong to such a solidary group even if they reject some self-designated spokesmen.

2. *Treatment as a group by others.* When members are treated by others as part of the same group and when others view them as being affected in a common way by political decisions, their solidarity will be promoted. The existence of

a formal organization promoting the interests of the solidary group increases the likelihood of such treatment by others. The creation of a government department to deal with a set of potential partisans as an identifiable constituency is an example of such recognition.

_3._ *A common style of life, norms, and values.* When members share a common subculture, solidarity will be enhanced. In such a situation, failure to uphold the interests of the group by a member will be met with sanctions on the part of other members—for example, with expressions of contempt such as "Uncle Tom" or "quisling." A formal organization promoting the interests of the solidary group may become an important vehicle for such sanctions.

_4._ *A high rate of interaction.* When members of the aggregate are geographically separated from others, when they have a significantly greater amount of social interaction with each other than with nonmembers, solidarity will be enhanced. Formal organizations composed of members of the solidary group perform the same sort of function and can mitigate the effects of geographical separation of members.

Solidary groups, then, are an important unit of potential partisan groups. Interest groups are the formally organized manifestations of solidary groups. They may serve as the vehicle for the exercise of influence by such groups and, in addition, they perform important functions in building and maintaining the solidarity of their constituency and in creating potential influence in such a constituency.

THE POTENTIAL PARTISAN-AUTHORITY RELATIONSHIP

It is now possible to state more precisely the relationship between potential partisans and authorities and its connections with influence and social control. Authorities are the recipients or targets of influence and the agents or initiators of social control. Potential partisans have the opposite roles—as agents or initiators of influence and targets or recipients of social control. Thus, the influence and social control relationships are the inverse of each other.[2]

Those without authority may also be the target of influence. If the relevant authorities for a given decision are dominated by a powerful group, this powerful group becomes a logical place to exert pressure. If someone can move this powerful group, he in turn becomes a likely recipient of influence and so on *ad infinitum*. The influence process involves a chain of such relationships but the chain ends with the authorities. Those earlier gatekeepers in the influence chain may also be authorities if there is a decision chain (as in the example above of the passage of a federal law) and their action is necessary before the final decision is binding.

The term "authorities" as used here has no intended connotation of exclusiveness—it should not be read as a synonym for "elite" or "ruling class." There may be many social systems in which every member is an authority on many decisions and a partisan on many others. In a community, for example, many issues may be decided by referendum or popular election. For the choice of a mayor, for a decision on bonding a new school, for a charter revision which gives new authority to the city council, the authorities are the electorate. In an election, the candidates and their supporters are the partisans. In such situations, it is the authorities who are the many and the partisans, the few.

---

[2]This can be stated more formally. The relationships we are concerned with are the Cartesian product of all possible subsets of potential partisans (P) and authorities (A). The domain of the influence relationship (I) in $P \times A = [p/\exists a, pIa]$. The range of $I = [a/\exists p, pIa]$. The social control relationship (S) is the inverse of this in $P \times A$: its domain = $[a/\exists p, aSp]$ and its range = $[p/\exists a, aSp]$.

Stop !

3

Discontent and trust

Potential partisans do not try to influence the outcome of every decision. When they do attempt influence, some threaten the authorities they wish to influence while others use the soft voice of persuasion. An interaction between partisans and authorities may alter their relationship in ways that change the probability of future influence attempts. Authorities may attempt to control the influence of potential partisans in various ways and with various consequences for the future behavior of these partisans.

To understand the nature of these influence and social control processes, this chapter explores certain basic attitudes of potential partisans toward authorities. These attitudes fall roughly under the rubric of "discontent." Words such as distrust, alienation, dissatisfaction, disaffection, and their opposites such as confidence, support, allegiance, trust, and satisfaction also identify the class of attitudes that concerns us.

The relevant discontent has a political focus. Its object or target is some level of the political system although this may range from the incumbent authorities to the political institutions and their justifications, to the political community as a whole. These different objects require discussion but first we consider the nature of the underlying attitude.

THE TRUST DIMENSION

What is it?

Trust in the government is a political attitude. The term

political attitude usually connotes opinions on specific public
issues or, if something more general, a syndrome of attitudes
which can be characterized on a left-right dimension. There is
a vast literature on political attitudes of this type. The trust
dimension, however, refers to a more basic political orientation. Lane illustrates it very well in comparing the attitudes
of his small sample of respondents in "Eastport" with a time

... in American history when a substantial proportion of the population
had reason to believe that the governments in office were, from their
standpoints, untrustworthy . . . . [various groups] were able to muster
significant support . . . [with] slogans and programs [which] revealed
that many men thought that the government was not operated in their
interest and that it was not for them (Lane, 1962, pp. 473-74).

But most of his respondents today felt that government was
responsive to their will. "If they think of government as affecting their lives at all, these Eastport men think of it as giving benefits and protections" (Lane, 1962, p. 474). Whether
there is more of such political trust today than in the past remains an open question which Lane's data cannot help us answer but his contrasting descriptions illustrate the dimension
of political trust.

Lane's terms for the attitudes are political "alienation" and
political "allegiance." He writes

Political alienation refers to a person's sense of estrangement from the
politics and government of his society. It may be taken to mean a feeling that these public matters are not "my affairs," that the government
is not "my government," that the Constitution is not "my Constitution"—in this sense, a disidentification. It implies more than disinterest;
it implies a rejection (Lane, 1962, p. 161).

Similarly, Neumann (1957, p. 290) characterizes political
alienation as the "conscious rejection of the whole political
system."

Lane suggests three more specific attitudes which together
form the political alienation syndrome:

1. I am the object, not the subject of political life—I have no influence and do not participate. Politically, I speak in the passive voice.
2. The government is not run in my interest; they do not care about
me; in this sense, it is not my government.

3. I do not approve of the way decisions are made; the rules of the game are unfair, loaded, illegitimate; the Constitution is, in some sense, fraudulent (Lane, 1962, p. 162).

What Lane approaches through the concept of political alienation, Easton (1965) approaches through the broader concept of "support." By support, Easton means favorable orientation toward a person, group, goal, idea, or institution. Support may involve actions (overt support) or attitudes (covert support). Members of a political system may be classified along a covert support continuum.

At the high end of the continuum, we would place members who are so intensively supportive in their attitudes that they virtually obliterate themselves as independently acting persons. They would substitute the needs, ideals, and standards of the supported object for their own. . . . At the low end of the continuum we would find those whose support is extremely negative, those who feel the deepest hostility to a system and are most decisively disengaged (Easton, 1965, p. 163).

Dahl (1966) touches briefly on the trust dimension in discussing cultural differences between countries which he suggests may bear on patterns of political opposition. Orientation toward the political system, one aspect of the political culture of a country, may be "classified as allegiance, when attitudes, feelings, and evaluations are favorable to the political system; apathy or detachment, when attitudes, feelings, and evaluations are neutral rather than positive or negative; and alienation, when attitudes, feelings, and evaluations are unfavorable" (Dahl, 1966, p. 353).

Almond and Verba (1965) are also concerned with different feelings toward government and politics in different countries. They make an important distinction between "output affect" or "the kinds of expectations people have of treatment at the hands of government officials" and "input affect" or "the feelings people have both about those agencies and processes that are involved in the election of public officials and about the enactment of general public policies" (1965, pp. 63-64). Their "output alienates" are aware of the government and believe it should do things for people like themselves but also believe that the government is "indiffer-

ent to the interest of poor people, or is corrupt and responsive only to bribes or family connections" (Almond and
Verba, 1965, p. 50).

The concept of political alienation is broader than the trust
dimension and Almond and Verba suggest the difference in
their distinction between input and output alienation. Political alienation includes both an efficacy (or input) dimension
and a trust (or output) dimension. Work on a sense of political efficacy derives from the studies by Campbell and his colleagues (1954; 1960; 1966). Political efficacy is measured by
disagreement with such items as "People like me don't have
any say about what the government does," and "Voting is
the only way people like me can have any say about how the
government runs things." The efficacy dimension of political
alienation refers to people's perception of their ability to influence; the trust dimension refers to their perception of the
necessity for influence. Feelings of low efficacy and feelings
that the government is not being run in one's interest are, of
course, likely to be found together. If one feels he cannot
contribute significant inputs he is likely also to feel unhappy
with the outputs but this is an empirical hypothesis which
might prove false under some conditions (e.g., paternalism,
noblesse oblige). In any event, these two aspects of political
alienation can be conceptually distinguished and the trust dimension refers to beliefs about the *outputs* of the political
system.

Why is trust important?

Probably few need convincing that such political discontent
is important but it is important for two different reasons—one
from a social control and the other from an influence perspective.

Trust as the creator of collective power. "In wartime,"
Winston Churchill told his parliamentary critics during a cen-
sure debate, "if you desire service, you must give loyalty"
(Churchill, 1962, Vol. 4, p. 352). Others have urged the

necessity of the same exchange in peacetime. Parsons has made
the argument most directly and fully.[1] Authorities must necessarily make a series of decisions under conditions of uncer-
tainty. "Effectiveness, therefore, necessitates the capacity to
make decisions and to commit resources, *independently of
specific conditions prescribed in advance* . . . by some kind of
prior agreement" (Parsons, 1961, p. 52). In other words, for
authorities to be effective they must have a good deal of freedom to commit resources without the prior consent of those
who will be called on ultimately to supply those resources.
Such freedom to invest or spend the resources they have
"borrowed" from members allows leaders to generate additional resources and thus, in theory, provide the lenders with
a generous return in the form of public goods or increased resources.

Like economic firms, units specializing in political function are dependent on the return of the power they have 'spent' or 'invested'
through their decisions about the allocation of resources. This return,
analogous to that from consumers' spending, takes the form of the constituency's satisfaction or dissatisfaction with these decisions, and it
thus directly affects the leadership's capacity to make further commitments (Parsons, 1961, p. 53).

The effectiveness of political leadership, then, depends on
the ability of authorities to claim the loyal cooperation of
members of the system without having to specify in advance
what such cooperation will entail. Within certain limits, effectiveness depends on a blank check. The importance of trust
becomes apparent: the loss of trust is the loss of system power, the loss of a generalized capacity for authorities to commit
resources to attain collective goals.

Authorities may, of course, use such power unwisely and,
as a result, experience a loss of credit which reduces it. This
is well illustrated by the changed conditions of trust in the

---

[1]Blau (1964) also makes similar points about the generation of trust in social
exchange but does not apply it as explicitly to trust in government.

Johnson administration from 1964 to 1967. In the summer
of 1964 when the President's credit rating was high, he asked
and received from Congress a generalized grant of authority
in the form of the "Bay of Tonkin" resolution. Following an
ambiguous incident off the coast of North Vietnam, a trusting
Congress agreed to give the President a wide latitude in making military commitments in Southeast Asia. An overwhelming election victory in November, 1964, increased such latitude even further. At that point, the President had a virtually
unlimited capacity to make commitments. He might have
used his credit to extricate the United States from its involvement in Vietnam at that time. Doing this would have involved
some risks including the possibility of events which would
have made the administration vulnerable to opposition charges
of "appeasement" or "softness." However, the President's
high credit at this point might have made such risks tolerable
had he chosen this course. Instead, he used his extraordinary
latitude to make a full-scale commitment of U.S. military
forces and prestige to the prosecution of the war.

The consequence of such a choice was a heavy erosion of
trust which reduced the President's freedom of action substantially. Such a loss was indicated by congressional refusal
in the spring of 1967 to grant the President broad freedom to
make commitments in Latin America without prior congressional consultation and approval. Another rough but useful
indicator of the President's credit may be found in the percentage approving his conduct in response to the poll question, "Do you approve or disapprove of the way [the incum-
bent] is handling his job as President?" President Johnson's
poll ratings suffered a substantial drop in the years following
his decision to engage the United States as a full-scale bellig-
erent in Vietnam. How much the unpopularity of the Vietnam war contributed to this drop and how much was a result
of other actions is a matter of conjecture. The point here is
not the cause but the effect of such a loss of confidence. The
President became increasingly less free to take actions which
would remove past errors and conceivably restore his credit

rating. Thus, distrust breeds conditions for the creation of further distrust.

Just as an incumbent administration may suffer a loss of effectiveness through a decline in political trust toward his personal leadership, a set of authorities or regime may experience a similar decline. A well-functioning government is, like a well-functioning bank, " 'insolvent' at any given moment with respect to its formal obligations if there is insistence on their fulfillment too rapidly" (Parsons, 1964, p. 60). The decline of trust has the effect of encouraging groups to demand explicit fulfillment. The presentation of demands by one group stimulates their presentation by others. Thus, it is possible for the loss of trust to encourage a "deflationary" spiral akin to a run on the bank. Parsons points to such a process as an essential part of the dynamics of revolution. Furthermore, under conditions of acute discontent, the government may be forced to divert resources urgently needed to meet its existing commitments in order to manage social control problems. This simply decreases its general capacities further. Coleman suggests another possible source of deflation with similar consequences. He argues,

It may be useful, . . . to conceive of loyalty to country as a kind of commodity foundation upon which large accounts of trust [are] drawn. The trust [is] necessary in order that the country's work get done (as evidenced, for example, by the breakdown in State Department functioning when loyalty reviews were instituted [during the McCarthy era]). The run on the accounts of trust occurred when there was suddenly believed to be a weaker commodity foundation of loyalty than previously supposed (Coleman, 1963, p. 76).

Political trust, then, is a kind of "diffuse support" which "forms a reservoir of favorable attitudes or good will that helps members to accept or tolerate outputs to which they are opposed or the effect of which they see as damaging to their wants" (Easton, 1965, p. 273). When the supply in the reservoir is high, the authorities are able to make new commitments on the basis of it and, if successful, increase such support even more. When it is low and declining, authorities may find it difficult to meet existing commitments and to govern effectively.

Trust as the source of inactivity. If trust provides opportunities for authorities, it may provide problems for potential partisan leaders. The problems center around the conversion of potential influence into effective action and around what might be called the "apathy" problem. Inactivity or lack of concern may have different meanings. When local newspapers urge a citizen to vote for any candidate as long as he votes, they are urging an act of diffuse support for the regime. Nonvoting as a means of withholding such support has never been better expressed than in comedian Mort Sahl's advice to voters in the 1960 Presidential election to "Vote 'No,' and keep the White House empty for another four years."

One meaning nonparticipation may have, then, is an expression of political alienation. This interpretation is supported by evidence from many countries that nonvoters tend to be less educated, lower status, nonorganizational members and in other ways less integrated into the society than are voters.[2] However, there is also evidence that participation increases in times of crisis. "In Germany and Austria," Lipset points out (1960, p. 189), "the normally high turnout reached its greatest heights in 1932-33, in the last elections before the destruction of the democratic system itself." This suggests that some people were not participating earlier because they were satisfied with things then and began participating because they were upset and concerned. Apparently, inactivity can be a sign of confidence as well as alienation. Or it may simply be a sign of irrelevance of politics and government for many people much of the time.

The "apathy" problem, then, has a different meaning for authorities and potential partisans. For the former, it is related to diffuse support; for the latter, it is related to their ability to influence. High trust in authorities implies some

---

[2]Such evidence is summarized in a number of places including Lipset (1960) and Lane (1959).

lack of necessity for influencing them. From the standpoint of potential partisans, a loss of trust in authorities may mean that solidary group members become more politically active, join organizations and contribute increasing time and money to influencing authorities.

Interest groups face two simultaneous problems and must consider their actions in the light of both. On the one hand, they are concerned with influencing authorities and producing favorable policies. On the other hand, they must maintain, or in many cases, create the support of a constituency. In this latter objective, they are in some respects competing with authorities for the support of a constituency. If trust is sufficiently high, interest groups may appear to be unnecessary mediators of solidary group interests. Why put time, energy, and money into an organization aimed at influencing authorities if these men can already be counted on to be responsive to the group's needs? A loss of trust in authorities may have the consequence of increasing the resources of interest groups by making the necessity of using them to influence authorities more apparent to solidary group members.

The trust variable makes the relation between successful influence and building the support of a constituency a highly complicated one. In many cases, the two goals of interest groups are complementary, successful influence stimulating member support and increased support stimulating more effective influence. However, with a relatively unorganized constituency, the problem of mobilizing support is likely to dominate the concerns of the interest group and short-run influence may be willingly sacrificed to this goal. In such cases, defeats may actually be preferred to victories if they occur in ways that diminish trust in authorities and increase group solidarity and personal investment in interest groups.

This has been explicitly argued by some individuals actively engaged in efforts to organize the urban poor into community unions.

Organizers must always keep in mind that it is occasionally more important to lose on a specific issue or in a specific confrontation. If the first time Mrs. Jones . . . confronts the 'power structure' she wins, her reaction may be to become satisfied with her present level of effectiveness and power. But if she and her neighbors lose the first time, the next time they confront the same or a different official, they may well have doubled their people power (under proper motivation by an organizer) thus strengthening the power of the parent organization.[3]

The moral that "nothing succeeds like failure" is not intended but only the more modest one that effects on political trust of constituents may be, quite properly, a more important determinant of partisan group strategy under some circumstances than the likelihood of immediate influence on authorities.

Failure and frustration are frequently debilitating and demoralizing and increases in discontent can have an effect that is the opposite from mobilizing people. More specifically, a combination of high sense of political efficacy and low political trust is the optimum combination for mobilization—a belief that influence is both possible and necessary. But, as noted above, a sense of efficacy and trust do not vary independently and any group strategy must be judged in terms of its effects on both variables.

Finally, if one considers trust between the leaders of a solidary group and their constituency, the considerations of trust discussed above under the social control perspective are applicable. In fact, an analysis of the internal politics of a social movement treats the movement's leaders as "authorities" and the solidary group as potential partisans. The greater the trust which such partisans invest in their leaders, the greater the freedom of action and capacity of such leaders for influencing other groups. If solidary group members hold leaders responsible for failures or regard them as manipulative and seeking personal power, the effectiveness of the leaders in achieving group goals may be impaired in the same way as the effectiveness of other authorities is hurt by loss of trust.

---

[3] Quoted from an unpublished paper by a community organizer, Conrad E. Egan, "Relationships between Community Power Structure Research and Community Organization," (April, 1967), 28 pp.

The objects of trust

It is possible for individuals simultaneously to feel high confidence in political institutions and alienation toward the incumbents who man them. Political trust is best thought of as a differentiated attitude toward different levels of the political system. Easton (1965) suggests three general foci of political solidarity or support—the authorities, the regime, and the political community.[4] These objects of trust have increasing levels of inclusiveness—the regime includes the authorities but is more general and the political community includes the regime but is more general.

By political community, Easton means a group bounded together by a "political division of labor" (1965, p. 177). The term implies that a "group of persons are for one reason or another joined together in a common political enterprise" (1965, p. 176). One may withdraw support from a regime and maintain it in a political community. A revolutionary movement might aim at replacing an existing regime with a new order but wish to preserve the political community. A separatist movement, however, challenges the political community. A rebellion of a colony against its colonial ruler illustrates the withdrawal of support from the political community.

The regime as an object of political trust may be thought of as a set of political institutions and their justifications. Easton (1965) suggests three components of the regime: values or broad general principles, norms, and the authority structure. The values are pretty well described by the "public philosophy" of a regime, i.e., "any set of principles and criteria above and beyond the reach of government and statesmen by which the decisions of government are guided and justified (Lowi, 1967, p. 5). Examples of such principles in the United States are equality of opportunity, preservation of individual liberty, and responsiveness to majority sentiment.

[4]Mitchell (1962, p. 16) further differentiates objects of political support. "The objects of support consist of the political values the polity presumably attempts to honor and realize, the polity itself (structures), the laws that govern society, the leaders and other personnel who operate the polity and government, and the policies being pursued by specific governments."

In addition to these general principles, each regime has a set of operating rules which "specify the way in which members of a system are expected to behave in political life. . . . These are the ground rules for participating in all aspects of the political process" (Easton, 1965, p. 200). Finally, a regime has various structural arrangements for carrying out such procedures—for example, a parliament, a system of departments, a judicial system, and so forth. I shall use the term "political institutions" to include both structural arrangements and the formal and informal rules of operation.

One may attack the political institutions of a regime in terms of its own public philosophy. Thus, the progressives sought to use such institutional innovations as the direct primary, initiative, and referendum in maintaining that "the cure for democracy is more democracy." Their quarrel was with practices rather than principles. Smelser (1963) makes this difference explicit in distinguishing between "norm-oriented" and "value-oriented" social movements, depending on the "component of action" which a movement wishes to restore, protect, modify, or create. Similarly, the public philosophy of a regime and its specific political institutions will be treated here as analytically independent objects of trust.

The final object of political support is the authorities themselves, the present incumbents of authority roles. Clearly, one can reject a particular administration while remaining confident in the political rules and institutions. All that is necessary is some tolerance or expectation of normal "error" in political institutions and a belief that they contain built-in provisions for correcting errors. Thus, a person may feel that a well-functioning political system will, in the manner of a good thermostat, occasionally produce too hot or too cold a temperature but there is no reason to replace it if such outputs are short-lived and self-correcting.

The generalization of political trust

Four objects of political trust are suggested here—the incumbent authorities, the political institutions of a regime, the public philosophy of a regime, and the political community. They may be considered hierarchical, each being a generalization of trust attitudes at the previous level. Potential partisans may be dissatisfied with the outcome of a given decision and not generalize it at all. Where there is a reservoir of high trust, many will feel that "Honest men may disagree and one cannot expect to win every time." In communities with high trust, the losers on a particular issue frequently claim to be satisfied with the decision in spite of their defeat because "We had a chance to be heard and point out the objections but we just weren't able to convince them."[5]

The dissatisfaction begins to be generalized when an undesirable outcome is seen as a member of a class of decisions with similar results. Authorities represent the first target of such generalization. Several unhappy outcomes or even one which is important enough to a group of potential partisans may lead them to the conclusion that the authorities are biased against them. If such experiences extend over more than one set of authorities, potential partisans may conclude that the institutions themselves may be the source of bias, and "throwing the rascals out" will have little effect if indeed it is even possible.

Attacks on political institutions may in turn lead to distrust in the ideology or public philosophy used to justify them. Thus some critics of contemporary American political institutions attack the particular form of "liberalism" which justifies these institutions. The term liberalism is usually given an appropriate modifier such as "interest-group liberalism" (Lowi, 1967) or "corporate liberalism" (Oglesby, 1965). Oglesby charges,

Corporate liberalism performs for the corporate state a function quite like what the Church once performed for the feudal state. It seeks to justify its burdens and protect it from change. As the Church exaggerated this office in the Inquisition, so with liberalism in the McCarthy time—which, if it was a reactionary phenomenon, was still made possible by our anti-Communist corporate liberalism (Oglesby, 1965).

---

[5]The quotation is from a respondent in a study of 18 New England communities reported in W. Gamson (1965; 1966a; 1966b).

Finally, if the institutions and the public philosophy maintain the unalterable allegiance of dominant and identifiable groups within the existing political community, the disaffection may be generalized to the political community itself and a desire for political separation may develop.

I am not arguing that the above process of generalization of political attitudes inevitably or even ordinarily takes place. Various sorts of inequalities may occur without their being regarded as a fault of the political system which may be structured so that it encourages or discourages the process of generalization. To discourage it, larger issues must be broken up into a series of smaller ones whenever this is possible. Roger Fisher (1964, p. 100) suggests such a strategy for stabilizing international conflicts. "Recognizing where possible that a dispute involves a question of the *application* of principle rather than the central principle itself should make it possible to decrease the stakes." By de-emphasizing the precedent setting aspects of decisions and by emphasizing their *ad hoc* nature, by deciding issues in bits and pieces rather than taking them in omnibus form, authorities can reduce the tendency for their decisions to lead to attitudes of confidence or alienation toward increasingly more general political objects. By the same token, a partisan group may wish to emphasize the symbolic aspects of an issue and be adverse to having decisions made in such a way that no new principle or precedent is established. They may do this precisely because they are anxious to promote attitudes of alienation which can be used to mobilize the group for further action.

There are also social structural conditions which encourage or discourage the generalization of political trust. The major variable here is the superimposition or overlapping nature of solidary group memberships. If members of a given solidary group are members of many other different groups with widely varying experiences with the political system, they will be less likely to generalize their attitudes from experiences with a single group. If, on the other hand, there is little overlap in membership between groups with different trust attitudes, the tendency to generalize such attitudes will be strengthened.

SOLIDARY GROUP TRUST

Solidary groups were described above as collections of individuals who think in terms of the effect of political decisions on the aggregate and feel that they are in some way personally affected by what happens to the aggregate. Feeling that they are affected in the same way by the political system, they are likely to develop similar attitudes of trust toward different political objects. On any given issue, the question of whether a solidary group is united or divided is an open one; nothing in the definition of such groups should be construed as resolving such questions. A single major issue on which the group is solidly united may sustain some shared attitude of common fate through many smaller issues on which the group is split. I will assume, however, that solidary group members occupy a similar position on basic attitudes of political trust. If this assumption is valid, it makes sense to characterize the group as a whole as possessing particular attitudes of trust in spite of some degree of variance among its members.

The political trust of a solidary group is its perception of the efficiency of the political system in achieving collective goals and its bias in handling conflicts of interest. The issues of fairness and efficiency are difficult to disentangle since most groups have a very strong tendency to rationalize their own interests as public interests. We can all be grateful to former Secretary of Defense Charles Wilson for making this assumption so explicit in his often quoted statement that he "always thought what was good for our country was good for General Motors, and vice versa." Such assumptions are widespread but typically unspoken.

A favorable bias in the political system, if it exists, is rarely defined as bias by those groups who are its beneficiaries. Instead, the tendency is to ignore the allocative aspects of decisions by treating the issues as technical problems which have more or less efficient solutions. It is a widely and sincerely held belief of many small town merchants that what is good for Main Street is good for their town. Indeed, it is undeniable that business interests are generally complementary with such

collective goals as the town's economic growth and the broad-
ening of its tax base. The suggestion that private aims are being justified or masked in the pursuit of such public goals
would be met with genuine indignation because the distinction
is not seen by those involved in such "civic" efforts.

Given the difficulty of disentangling a group's perceptions
of fairness from its perceptions of efficiency, it is desirable to
define trust in a way that combines the two dimensions. This
can be done by defining a "preferred" outcome for a solidary
group as the one it regards as most favorable to its interests
when they conflict with other groups *or* as the most efficient
for the system as a whole. Its political trust can be defined as
the probability, P_b, that the political system (or some part of
it) will produce preferred outcomes even if left untended. In
other words, it is the probability of getting preferred outcomes without the group doing anything to bring them about.
They or others may do things to influence this probability but
one can measure such alterations against the baseline of P_b.

Any solidary group may be characterized by a particular
value (or range of values) of P_b. These values are continuous,
of course, but it will be useful in discussing political trust to
describe three pure points of *confidence, neutrality,* and
alienation.

Confidence

Confidence is the belief that for any given decision, $P_b = 1.0$.
Confidence in authorities means that they are perceived as the
group's agents, that the group members identify with them.
This would be true if one were fulfilling the authority role
oneself; it is approximated by having members or one's solidary group in such roles. Confidence in the political institutions means that the group believes either that these institutions produce authorities who are its agents or else produce
favorable decisions regardless of the particular incumbents.
Confidence in the public philosophy means that the group
believes that this philosophy fosters and maintains a set of

institutions in which it has confidence. Confidence in the political community means that the group believes such a community fosters and maintains a public philosophy and set of political institutions in which it has confidence.

Neutrality

Neutrality is the belief that for any given decision, $P_b = 0.5$. There are different processes by which one can arrive at this state of neutrality. It may involve a view of the political system as composed of highly variable and erratic objects, potent but unpredictable in producing preferred outcomes. The authorities, for example, may be seen as highly dependent on influence with little a priori tendency in any direction. Alternatively, there may be little salience to political objects. The group may perceive the political system as a neutral feature of the landscape. Like the roads and rivers about one, it performs some useful functions but is too much in the background for the group to have developed expectations about its probability of producing preferred outcomes on decisions which affect them. No expectations are equivalent to neutrality. Finally, members of a solidary group may be members of other solidary groups as well. If the different groups to which they belong have variable experiences with the political system—a mixture of positive and negative ones—then the group's political trust will reflect this balance.

Neutrality toward authorities means that the group believes that such authorities are moderately competent and efficient in achieving collective goals but that they offer no special leadership skills. The authorities do as well, in this belief, as any set of citizens picked at random. The belief that they have relevant experience, training, or wisdom, which enables them to perform with better than average skill reflects confidence rather than neutrality. On questions of conflict, a solidary group with a neutral attitude regards the authorities as indifferent and disinterested. The outcome is dependent on what happens in the situation and on the application of certain general standards of equity but there is no built-in disposition toward any party in the conflict.

Neutrality toward political institutions means that the group sees such institutions as one among many arrangements for achieving collective goals. They have no special sanctity and embody no special wisdom. They serve to do the job but with no special distinction. On questions of conflict, the institutions are regarded as fair. They are like a civil court in which neither plaintiff nor defendant has any special advantage. The rules allow for a fair fight.

Neutrality toward the public philosophy means that the group sees such a philosophy as fostering no specific set of political institutions or else fostering neutral ones. It is not regarded as an ideology by which a dominant group "gives its ideas the form of universality and [tries] to represent them as the only rational and universally valid ones" (Marx, 1956, p. 80). Rather it is a set of abstractions with no particular implications for specific political institutions. Neutrality toward the political community means that the group takes the existing community boundaries as a neutral fact of life fostering no particular public philosophy and political institutions or else fostering neutral ones.

Alienation

Alienation is the belief that for any given decision, $P_b = 0$. Alienation from authorities means that they are regarded as incompetent and stupid in achieving collective goals and biased against the group in handling conflicts of interest. They are antiagents of the group, the agents of groups with conflicting goals. "The alienated man," writes Lane (1962, p. 171) "not only believes that government is failing to serve his interest; he believes that it is also serving some other set of interests, either those of a rival class or of the 'vested interests' or of some hostile, disliked, rejected group."

Alienation toward political institutions means that the group believes either that such institutions put its foes in office or that they are rigged against preferred outcomes regardless of who the incumbents are. Alienation toward the public philosophy means that the group believes that such a philosophy fosters and maintains a set of political institutions from which it is alienated. Alienation toward the political community means that the group believes that the existing community fosters and maintains a public philosophy and political institutions from which they are alienated.

Optimum degree of solidary group trust

From our earlier discussion of trust as the creator of collective power, it would appear that from the standpoint of the authorities, the more trust the better. However, if every solidary group in a political system were confident, there would be something amiss. Since groups have different preferred outcomes on many issues, some would have to be either ignorant or deluded.

Such misplaced confidence may be welcomed by authorities and in relatively closed and totalitarian political systems, there could conceivably be a stable state of delusion. In a more open system, however, it is likely to be a potential source of instability. With such a fragile foundation for trust, there is always a danger of a sudden collapse of credit and it may come at a time when the government has heavy commitments and can ill afford it. The more accurate the perceptions of the political process by solidary groups, the greater is the likelihood that highly confident groups will have alienated counterparts. In short, on issues which involve conflict of interest, there is a more stable foundation if solidary groups perceive the system as neutral, i.e., as unbiased.

This is not true with respect to the efficiency of the political system. The existence of high confidence for one part of the population need not imply less confidence for any other part. Since solidary group attitudes are an amalgam of beliefs about bias and efficiency, the ideal trust orientation for any group is neutrality on questions of bias and confidence on

questions of efficiency. This leaves its resultant trust some-
where in between at a position of moderate confidence. In a
well-functioning political system, the set of all solidary groups
should be characterized by moderate confidence on the average and low variance in political trust between groups. The
average trust may be regarded as a measure of the efficiency
of a system while the variance between groups is a measure of
its fairness. Thus, the political system in a society in which
average trust is quite high but variance in trust between different groups is also substantial is doing well in the achievement
of collective goals but has problems of equity in distribution.
One in which average trust is relatively low but more or less
equal between groups is like the man in the New Yorker car-
toon who announces that he hates everyone regardless of
race, creed, or national origin: in such a system, every group
gets its fair share of misery. This discussion is elaborated below
in the section of Chapter 8 on "Social Control and Trust." At
that point, we will consider specific hypotheses on the type
of action that authorities will adopt toward groups with different trust orientations.

4

Influence in use

Any discussion of power and influence is hampered by the fact that no established consensus on terminology exists. Some writers, for example, distinguish the terms power and influence while others use them interchangeably. As used here, power refers both to authorities operating on potential partisans and to the reverse operation. I will use the term social control when I wish to speak of what authorities do to potential partisans, and influence to cover the reverse. Influence is the family name for an array of connected concepts and this chapter identifies the members and tries to clarify their kinship relations.

The task has already begun through specifying the agents and targets of influence: potential partisans and authorities. This hardly reduces the number of people involved since authorities are more than simply government officials. Almost everyone makes binding decisions at some level of social organization, be it community, voluntary association, work organization, family, or some other. But while defining authorities as the target of influence does not reduce who is involved, it does circumscribe the behavior being influenced. Many kinds of influence are beyond the scope of this book: influence on attitudes and values and on various actions are of concern only when they affect the binding choices of people acting in an authority role.

THE NATURE OF INFLUENCE

What is the nature of this influence that partisans attempt

to exercise over authorities? It is a special case of behavioral effects. Simon (1957, p. 5) puts it in terms of causality. "The statement 'A has power over B' is equivalent to the statement 'A causes B's behavior.' " This is an extremely broad concept of influence, omitting as it does any idea of A's intention. But it underlines the fact that A must be at least partially determining B's behavior, altering it from what it would have been in A's absence.

There is a story about a man, who, early each morning, enthusiastically threw bits of newspaper in the street. One morning, a woman who had watched this performance for several months approached him and asked him what he was doing. "I'm throwing this paper down to keep the elephants out of the streets," he replied. "But there are no elephants in the streets," she reproached him. "That's right! he said triumphantly, "Effective, isn't it."

Fundamental to the idea of influence then, is the requirement that the decision-making behavior of authorities has been altered from what it would have been in the absence of the influencer. To conceive of influence as a shift in the probability of an outcome is one of Dahl's (1957) several outstanding contributions to this area.[1] Assume that a particular potential partisan group does nothing to influence the outcome of a given decision and that the authorities do not know the group's preferred outcome. We have already (in Chapter 3) introduced a term to cover this situation: P_b, or the probability that the political system will produce preferred outcomes without the group doing anything to bring them about. This may be thought of as the probability before or without influence. But assume that our group becomes active and does various things which alter P_b. The new probability of obtaining the preferred outcome after influence attempts have

---

[1]Weber (1947, p. 152) long ago spoke of "the probability that one actor within a social relationship will be in a position to carry out his will despite resistance . . ." in his definition of "power" (*Macht*). This is not at all the same, however, as defining power as a *change* in probability conditional on the actions of the influencer.

occurred will be called, P_a. *A partisan group can be said to have exercised influence if and only if there is a difference between P_a and P_b.*

Operationalizing influence

This simple and appealing definition has an array of operational and conceptual problems. There are three approaches to the operational difficulties.

1. *The relative frequency approach.* Since there is no meaningful way of talking about the "objective" probability of a single event, one can restrict statements about the exercise of power to classes of similar decisions. An operational index of influence is then provided by subtracting the frequency of obtaining a particular outcome when a partisan group works against it from the frequency when it works in favor of it. For example, one can examine the relative frequency of (say) a foreign policy bill passing when Senator X works in favor of it and the relative frequency of it passing when he works against it. If the first probability is substantially higher, then Senator X can be said to exercise substantial influence on foreign policy decisions.

Such an index of influence runs into serious difficulties if one must use, as a matter of convenience, the senator's recorded vote as a measure of his activities prior to the vote. As Dahl (1957) emphasizes in using such a measure, it becomes impossible to distinguish the genuine influencer from the "chameleon." "Suppose," Dahl asks (1957, pp. 212-13), "a Senator takes no prior position on any bill and always decides how to vote by guessing how the Senate majority will vote; then, if he is a perfect guesser [he will appear to be exercising maximum possible influence when he is, in fact, exercising none]." A close relative of the chameleon is the "satellite," the senator who religiously follows the dictates of a powerful colleague but exercises no independent influence of his own. He would appear to be exercising the same influence as his colleague when, in fact, he was only reflecting such influence.

MacRae and Price (1959) suggest still another source of spurious influence.

> It results from the fact that legislators often cast roll-call votes so as to locate themselves along a one-dimensional continuum in a given subject matter area (e.g., foreign policy or taxation). . . . Insofar as this is true, those legislators nearest the median of the distribution of legislators along this continuum will necessarily have the highest indices [of influence by the operational definition being discussed] " (MacRae and Price, 1959, p. 213).

In this case, the more "representative" the senator is of senatorial sentiment, the more influence he will appear to have even when he is exercising none.

Such criticisms of a particular index may lead to undue pessimism about operational difficulties. The problems above are far from insoluble; they require only that one have some measure of actual partisan activity prior to a vote rather than relying on the vote itself as a measure of this. Dahl suggests that "observations of this kind are available only with great difficulty" (1957, p. 214) but the difficulties seem no greater than for myriad other research situations in which information must be painfully gathered through interviews and observations rather than simply plucked from the pages of *Congressional Quarterly* or from some other volume in the reference room of the nearest library.

One existing study does correlate prior partisan activity with decision outcomes. I am hesitant to say how successful it is in operationalizing the concept of influence since it is my own (W. Gamson, 1966b). This study examined the influence of "reputational leaders" in 18 New England communities over a set of 54 issues. The basic strategy involved assessing the partisan activity of reputational leaders on each issue and determining on which ones there was some degree of both activity and unity by the set of reputational leaders in a community. On such issues, it was then possible to ask whether the side supported by the reputational leaders was more likely to win than the other side. It turns out that when the reputational leaders were active and united, they won about 75 percent of the time.

However, it is not enough to look only at whether reputational leaders were on the winning or losing side for two reasons. First, one cannot assume that the a priori probability of winning (i.e., P_b) was 0.5. Perhaps it was already 0.75 for the proposals supported by the reputational leaders; if so, we need hardly be impressed that they were on the winning side 75 percent of the time. In the study of New England communities, the asymmetry of the influence task for different partisan groups was assumed. "Those on one side of an issue are likely to have a natural advantage over those on the other side, an advantage which will enable them to win if they simply hold their own in an influence contest" (Gamson, 1966b, p. 122).

This natural advantage is the advantage that falls to those who do not carry the burden of proof. In relatively stable systems, this advantage is held by those who would maintain a present arrangement against those who would alter it.

Many community issues arise from the presentation of a proposal to alter some existing facility or service or to add some new facility. The burden of proof in such cases generally rests with the side proposing the change. For example, if a new school is proposed, those who oppose it may raise any number of questions about need, cost, design, site, and so forth. It is not necessary to resolve such questions in order to block action on this proposal; if they remain unanswered, this is generally sufficient (W. Gamson, 1966b, p. 122).

On 48 of the issues studied, it was possible to identify one side with an effort to change the status quo in some fashion while the other side favored postponement of action, further study of need, a counter alternative requiring less change, or simply the maintenance of existing arrangements. The side identified with change was victorious 42 percent of the time against 58 percent for those who opposed the immediate action proposed. This figure of 42 percent cannot be taken as a measure of P_b because it includes the influence of campaigns by both sides. If one side made a more effective effort this is presumably reflected in an improved probability of victory. Since such efforts tended to be greater on the part of those supporting change, it is reasonable to assume that the P_b for the side desiring change is less than 0.42.

One factor one must consider, then, in determining whether reputational leaders exercised influence is the value of P_b. A second factor is the contribution of other influences. An attempt was made to capture this through a measure of overall campaign effort by the two sides. The winning side, it turns out, had only a modest advantage in campaign effort: on 48 percent of the issues, it waged the more vigorous campaign while the losing side made a larger effort on 33 percent of the issues. On the remainder, the two sides were essentially equal in effort.

The extent of a priori advantage for the side supporting the status quo can be seen even more clearly when the relative campaign efforts are considered. As Table 1 shows, in almost two thirds of the cases in which the side supporting change won, they made a greater campaign effort than the other side. However, when the side supporting the status quo won, they made a greater effort only a third of the time; two thirds of the time they were able to win with no more effort than the losing side.

With the variables of campaign effort (i.e., the influence contributions of others) and of status quo advantage (i.e., P_b) identified, we are in a better position to assess whether reputational leaders have exercised influence. Campaign effort is a conservative control—one which underestimates the influence of reputational leaders—because some of the activity may have been contributed by the reputational leaders. Nevertheless, it turns out that reputational leader support means a higher frequency of victory than reputational leader opposition over and above the effects of the two control variables. Reputational leaders have as high a proportion of victories when they support a side with equal or less-campaign effort as when they support the side with more effort. Furthermore,

TABLE 1

Campaign Effort and Success in Changing the Status Quo for 52
Issues in 18 New England Communities*

Winning Side	Supported Change		Supported Status Quo		Change Issue Irrelevant
	%	(N)	%	(N)	(N)
Made greater campaign effort . . .	65	(13)	32	(9)	(3)
Made same campaign effort. . . .	10	(2)	29	(8)	(0)
Made smaller campaign effort . . .	25	(5)	39	(11)	(1)
Total (N = 52) .	100	(20)	100	(28)	(4)

*This table is reproduced from W. Gamson (1966b, p. 127). The base for these figures is 52 rather than 54 issues since 2 were excluded because of ambiguity over the outcome which made it impossible to designate the winning side.

they achieve their success *against* the natural advantage gained from supporting the status quo; they are successful in support of change two thirds of the time.

This study of the influence of reputational leaders in community politics operationalizes influence in the manner suggested by Dahl. Since the relative frequency of an alternative passing was higher when reputational leaders were behind it than when they opposed it and since this difference existed over and above the effects of total campaign activity and the "natural advantage" of the status quo, reputational leaders can be said to have exercised influence in the communities studied.

2. *The subjective probability approach.* Frequently we want to make statements about the exercise of influence on a

single issue. For example, we may want to say whether President Johnson's skill in handling Congress increased the probability that the Civil Rights Act of 1964 would pass over the probability that it would have passed if President Kennedy had lived. Or, to take another example, we may want to know whether the opposition of various groups in the United States to the administration's conduct of the war in Vietnam "had any influence" over the probability of various policy decisions. One cannot conclude that no influence has occurred simply by a failure to achieve a preferred outcome. A partisan group may start with little chance of a policy being accepted but by waging a vigorous fight, it may reach a point where acceptance of the policy is touch and go. Perhaps in the end the group loses, but the change from almost certain failure to a near-miss is a mark of its influence.

The theoretical definition of influence as the difference between P_a and P_b is still useful in talking about influence on a single event. However, we must abandon *objective* probability as a way of operationalizing influence on a single event, and substitute *subjective* probability. What odds would a set of informed observers give on the outcome of the decision before and after the relevant acts of influence occurred? If the preferred alternative is now a "better bet," then we can say that influence has occurred. For example, if a bill is given one chance in four of passing the Senate by experienced and informed observers before Senator X takes a stand and is given two chances in three of passing after Senator X has waged a vigorous campaign on its behalf, we can say that Senator X has influenced the decision. The actual outcome is irrelevant to this operational definition which measures influence by a shift in subjective probability. Of course, one must deal with the reliability and validity of the observers' judgments but there are standard techniques for dealing with such problems.[2]

---

[2]See, for example, J. P. Guilford, *Psychometric Methods* (New York: McGraw-Hill Book Co., 1954), for an extended discussion of such techniques.

3. *The influence attempt approach.* The final approach to operationalizing influence involves an end run. Instead of examining influence, one examines two other related concepts: influence attempts and capability of influence. Influence attempts are considerably easier to measure than is influence since one only needs to look at the behavior of partisans without worrying about the response of authorities. Rosenau (1961) takes this approach in his examination of public opinion and foreign policy. He substitutes for the difficult concept of influence a more manageable one: "the transmission of opinion." "Thus, by distinguishing and classifying the various participants in the opinion-policy relationship according to the form which their communicative behavior takes, it should be possible to avoid the difficulties of measuring influence . . . " (Rosenau, 1961, p. 16).

If we can understand the process of influence attempts and can then combine it with some measure of capability, we may move far toward inferring influence without measuring it. Capability is handled by the concept of *resources,* and is discussed at length below. The influence attempt approach involves making one central assumption: the possession of resources plus the existence of influence attempts implies influence. This assumption cannot be tested without using one of the direct measures of influence suggested above. However, if it is accepted as reasonable or established by evidence, one can then proceed to study influence by measuring influence attempts and the distribution of resources without ever attempting to assess influence directly.

Each of these approaches to an operational definition of influence is viable and appropriate for particular situations. When MacRae and Price (1959, p. 218) conclude that "Although the conceptualization of [influence] has been advanced [by Dahl], the operational definition of it has not yet been accomplished," they react too much to the faults of one particular operational definition. In fact, the operational problems seem manageable enough.

Theoretical problems in defining influence

A major theoretical problem is created by the fact that when one group attempts influence, it frequently stimulates similar action from other, opposing groups. Suppose, for example, that a civil rights group wishes a city council to pass an Open Housing Ordinance and that a group of citizens on the north side of town fear such an ordinance. The northsiders regard the ordinance as unlikely to pass and, therefore, plan little activity against it. If and only if the civil rights group becomes active will the northsiders become active on the other side. For the sake of argument, assume that the activity of the northsiders always is exactly enough to neutralize the actions of the civil rights group. Thus, P_a is the same as P_b in spite of a vigorous campaign by the civil rights group. Must we say that they have had no influence on this decision?

One might be tempted to see this as a measurement difficulty rather than a conceptual one. A theoretical solution might be found by assigning the effects to the immediate actions of the civil rights group regardless of any future action by the northsiders. This would then be a case in which the council was influenced in one direction by the civil rights group and then later influenced back to the starting point by their opponents. Unfortunately, this will not suffice. First, the northsiders' action was not *independent;* it was contingent on the first group's action. Second, the civil rights group may have exercised influence by galvanizing other supporting groups—for example, the Ministerial Alliance which would have remained quiet had they not been prodded. If future actions that are conditional on the group's activity are to be included, then we must include both the ministers' wanted action and the northsiders' unwanted action.

It seems necessary, then, to define influence in terms of *net effects.* If the civil rights group produced reactions which offset its influence attempts, then it exercised no influence. One must be able to attribute the effect to the group in question. We cannot conclude that the civil rights group exercised no influence over the city council unless we know that the actions of the northsiders were contingent on those of the civil rights group. It may be that they would have launched a campaign against the Open Housing Ordinance in any event. If their actions are not conditional, if they represent no "backlash," their impact cannot be considered part of the net effect of the actions of the civil rights group. The net effect of a group's presence and its actions includes only the *contingent* actions of other groups.

Influence can occur without any current action on the part of the potential partisan group. If a federal civil rights bill is changed or not introduced in the first place because of fears of a Southern filibuster in the Senate, then it is not unreasonable to say that the Southern senators have affected the probability of the passage of the civil rights bill *even if no filibuster has occurred.* Nor need a Southern spokesman warn the Justice Department that a filibuster will occur or even make a veiled and implicit threat to this effect. The very existence of a rule allowing unlimited debate in the Senate and a group that has used it on certain specified occasions in the past and can do so again, is enough to create the influence.

To restate the definition of P_b and P_a in a form that incorporates these points, P_b is the probability that a preferred alternative will be passed if the potential partisan group can or will take *no action* contingent on what the authorities propose to do. P_a is the net result of the addition of the potential partisan group to the situation. Influence has occurred if there is a difference between P_a and P_b regardless of whether the potential partisan group has taken some action. Of course, the amount of influence may vary if the group acts in one way rather than another. In many cases, there may be no difference between P_a and P_b *unless* the group takes some action.

It is worth noting that this definition of influence which is drawn so heavily from Dahl, violates one of the two *necessary* conditions which he suggests must be present before influence can be said to exist.

A necessary condition for the power relation is that there exists a time lag, however small, from the actions of the actor who is said to exert power to the responses of the respondent. This requirement merely accords with one's intuitive belief that A can hardly be said to have power over a unless A's power attempts precede a's responses. . . . Who runs the XYZ Corporation? Whenever the president announces a new policy, he immediately secures the compliance of the top officials. But upon investigation it turns out that every new policy he announces has first been put to him by the head of the sales department (Dahl, 1957, p. 204).

It is possible, however, that the head of the sales department is careful to suggest only those alternatives that he believes will be supported by the chairman of the board of directors. In the absence of this gentleman, he would not propose a particular alternative and the president would not accept it if he did. The probability of its adoption would be greatly altered. Are we then correct in attributing all the influence to the head of the sales department who has taken some action rather than allocating some to the chairman of the board whose presence has changed the probability of the policy being adopted perhaps even more?

Dahl suggests a second necessary condition which can be more fully accepted. "Unless there is some 'connection' between A and a, then no power relation can be said to exist. . . . In looking for a flow of influence . . . from A to a, one must always find out whether there is a connection, or an opportunity for a connection, and if there is not, then one need proceed no further" (1957, p. 204). If the head of the sales department asked himself how Jomo Kenyatta or the Queen of England would feel about the policy, no influence would be attributed to them. No matter how important they are as figures of identification, they are not present in the situation in the same sense that the chairman of the board is. While there need not necessarily *be* an action by the influencer, there must be the possibility for action. The influencer must be able and likely to know how the authorities will act and be able to respond to their actions. Interaction is a necessary condition of influence.

SOME CONCEPTS IN THE INFLUENCE FAMILY

Negative Influence

Intentionality is imbedded in the definition of influence through the concept of a preferred outcome. Groups may also do various things which affect outcomes inadvertently. Such effects constitute influence only when they involve *preferred* outcomes. "Any reciprocal contact between human beings leads to the modification of the actions of the participants," Easton argues (1953, p. 143). "If [influence] is so broadly conceived, then every relation is an illustration of [an influence] situation. . . . To give [influence] any differentiated meaning we must view it as a relationship in which one person or group is able to determine the actions of another in the direction of the former's own ends."

Actions must affect preferred outcomes to be considered influence but what if they affect them in an unintended direction? Is it influence if the actions of a group make P_a lower than P_b instead of higher as the group intended? Dahl (1957, p. 205) suggests that we might call this "negative" influence. "If whenever I ask my son to stay home on Saturday morning to mow the lawn, my request has the inevitable effect of inducing him to go swimming, when he would otherwise have stayed home, I do have a curious kind of negative [influence] over him."

This negative influence may be produced in two basic ways. First, a group may, by its actions, create resistance on the part of authorities. Cartwright (1959) and French and Raven (1959) have pointed to a distinction between "opposition to an influence attempt" and "resistance generated by an influence attempt." Opposition is based on the content of the proposed policy. "In resistance the content is quite secondary and may even be irrelevant" (Cartwright, 1965, p. 34). Resistance may lead authorities to "punish" a group by withholding preferred outcomes and to protect and reward the group's adversaries. It is in this sense that civil rights groups frequently have regarded some of their cruder enemies

as assets for their cause. A clumsy influence attempt will produce negative influence when the resistance it generates makes
P_a lower than P_b.

The second way in which negative influence occurs is
through activating other potential partisan groups with opposing objectives. "White backlash," for example, seems to
mean anti-Negro and anticivil rights activity, stimulated by
the influence attempts of Negroes and their allies. To give the
term a more general meaning, *backlash* is the counterinfluence
of opposing groups which is *conditional* on the influence
activity of a given partisan group. It should not be confused
with the influence activities of opposing groups when such
activities are partly or wholly *independent* of what the partisan group is doing and would have gone on in any event. The
backlash portion of such activity is that part which is contingent. A group has exercised negative influence if the impact of backlash activity outweighs the impact of the group's
own activity.

Amount of influence

The amount of influence exercised is simply the degree of
probability change in the desired direction. It is worth emphasizing again that defeat does not necessarily imply lack of
influence. This point is typically forgotten in the postmortem
that accompanies a political defeat. The losers will take themselves to task for various failures, assuming that their a priori
probability of winning was 0.5. The other side is seen as having spent more resources or as having used its resources more
efficiently. While this may be the case, not infrequently the
losing side exercises a large amount of influence while the
winning side does little or nothing to further their cause.

Basis of influence

The basis of influence refers to *what* is used and the means
to *how* it is used. What is it that a group uses to exercise

influence? In any decision, there exists some "thing" or "weight" such that if enough of this weight is applied to the authorities, P_b will be altered. Lasswell and Kaplan (1950, p. 83), define a "base value" as follows: "Whenever X has influence over Y, there is some value with regard to which X enjoys a favorable position, and because of which he can exercise influence over Y. This is the base value of the influence relation. . . . " A more natural term, and one which I shall use here, is *resource*. Thus, Dahl (1957, p. 203) writes that the "base of an actor's power consists of all the *resources*—opportunities, acts, objects, etc.—that he can exploit in order to effect the behavior of another."

Two important conditions must be satisfied before something can be called a resource. First, the thing must be possessed by, or more accurately, *controlled* by the influencer. He must be able to determine its use. Second, he must be able to bring it to bear on authorities in interaction with them. Something which is a resource with respect to one social system and one group of authorities will not necessarily be a resource for all systems and all authorities.

The concept of resources is elaborated in the discussions of potential influence and cost of influence below. At this point, a few examples are sufficient, but their justification is deferred. All of the following are resources in some situations: the ability to hire, promote and fire people; the ability to allocate corporation money to civic projects; the authority to make decisions on a variety of issues; the ability to influence large numbers of voters to withdraw their political support from an individual or project; the ability to enhance or damage reputation through control of some communication medium; the possession of a generalized reputation for wisdom on public affairs.

Means of influence

Knowing what resources a group controls does not tell us how it uses them. For example, a person with money might use it to bribe officials, to employ a private army which threatens them, or to publish and distribute a pamphlet setting forth the reasons why they should act in the desired fashion. A typology of means of influence tells us the different ways in which resources are used to influence authorities.

A large list of writers have distinguished types of influence.[3] Cartwright (1965) has an excellent systematic review of most of these discussions and no purpose is served by repeating such a review here. It is clear that there are many ways of classifying influence. Where one author carefully distinguishes between three or four means, another will ignore their differences and casually treat them as a piece. The particular distinctions employed are dictated by one's objectives and there are many valid typologies, each useful for specific purposes.

The classification of means used here is dictated by a desire to relate means of influence to political trust. It is based on two underlying dimensions:

1. *Situational versus orientational influence.* This distinction is made in a number of discussions, most explicitly by Parsons.

There is a very simple paradigm of means by which one acting unit ... can attempt to get results by bringing influence to bear on another unit. . . . The first variable is whether ego attempts to work through potential control over the *situation* in which alter is placed and must act, or through an attempt to have an effect on alter's *intentions* independently of changes in his situation (Parsons, 1963, pp. 42-43).

2. *Adding advantages versus adding disadvantages.* This distinction is a further breakdown of situational influence. It is important whether changes or promised changes in the situation are advantageous or disadvantageous to the authorities. As Thibaut and Kelley (1959, p. 105) point out, if the target of influence is "controlled solely by augmentation (say he is offered rewards for compliance), he will monitor himself. . . .

---

[3] A partial list includes French and Raven in Cartwright (1959); Kelman (1961); Etzioni (1961); Neumann (1950); Janowitz (1960); Goldhamer and Shils (1939); Harsanyi (1962); Parsons (1963); Rosenberg and Pearlin (1962); Gilman (1962); Russell (1938); and Thibaut and Kelley (1959).

In contrast, when reduction [e.g., punishment] . . . is threatened for noncompliance [the target's compliance must be
kept], under surveillance." Lasswell and Kaplan (1950, p. 97)
recognize the distinction in defining "constraint" and "inducement." "*Constraint*," they write, "is the exercise of influence
by threat of deprivation; *inducement*, by promise of indul-
gence."

These two dimensions, then, yield three means of influence.
They are outlined in Chart 1 with the labels used here: constraints, inducements, and persuasion.

CHART 1
Typology of Means of Influence

Underlying Dimensions	Addition of Disadvantages	Addition of Advantages
Changes in the situation of the authorities	Constraints	Inducements
Changes in the orientation of the authorities	Persuasion	

A. Constraints. Constraints are the addition of new disadvantages to the situation or the threat to do so, regardless
of the particular resources used. A student group threatening
to hold a sit-in unless the university administration takes a
desired course of action is using constraints. So is the U.S.
government when it drops "antipersonnel" bombs on North
Vietnam in an effort to make that government's participation
in the war in South Vietnam more "punishing."

It is important that the disadvantages be an *addition* to the
situation. Whether an act constitutes the addition of a disad-

vantage or an advantage is not always clear from the act itself. As Blau argues,

> The crucial factor is the baseline from which an individual starts when another seeks to influence him and the only difference between punishments and rewards is in relation to this initial baseline, whether he is worse or better off than he was before the transaction started. . . . A man who has reason to expect to remain in his job does not think of his regular earnings as distinctive rewards and the loss of his income is a punishment for him (Blau, 1964, pp. 116-17).

Imagine that the American Farm Bureau Federation told Senator X that they will support his reelection *if and only if* he votes against an impending farm bill. If we knew only this fact, we would not know whether punishment had been threatened or reward had been promised.

Thibaut and Kelley's concept of *comparison level* is helpful in dealing with the problem of the baseline. This is "a standard by which the person evaluates the rewards and costs of a given relationship in terms of what he feels he 'deserves' " (1959, p. 21). Thus, if Senator X has always been supported by the Farm Bureau and had every reason to expect their continued support, then their communication to him is a threat. If they had opposed him in the past and he had little reason to expect their support, then the statement is a promise of a new advantage. If Senator X had been unsure of Farm Bureau support, then the statement contains both a threat and a promise. In this case, it should be treated as two acts of influence: a threat that the Farm Bureau will support the Senator *only if* he votes against the bill and a promise that they will support him *if* he votes against it.

It is not necessarily a threat to warn authorities that if they follow a particular policy dire consequences will follow for them. It is simply an act of persuasion if the influencer has no control over whether these dire things will occur or not. To be a threat, the influencer must be the manipulator of the disadvantages, not merely a reporter of them. The civil rights leader who warns of riots if the problems of the urban ghetto are not adequately dealt with is not issuing a threat. But if he promises to denounce the relevant authorities personally and publicly for their "irresponsibility" if they fail to act, he is issuing a threat.

A threat is still a threat regardless of how gently it is worded. Since threats have a tendency to create resistance, they are typically veiled. If the Farm Bureau tells someone they have always supported, "We will support you if you help defeat this objectionable bill," they are telling him in a polite manner that their continued support is conditional. This is a tactfully worded threat.

B. Inducements. Inducements are the addition of new advantages to the situation or the promise to do so, regardless of the particular resources used. The authority acts as the partisan group desires in exchange for some resource which they have received or will receive. There is a specific good or service involved as a *quid pro quo* in such an exchange.

Social exchange has been used as a major theme and been given a very broad definition by some writers.[4] The "exchange" involved in inducements is intended to be much narrower so that it can be distinguished from persuasion which also involves an exchange in the broadest sense. Authorities may strongly desire the respect, admiration, and affection of some potential partisan group. If the partisan group expresses its wishes on some issue and the authorities meet these wishes in "exchange" for the group's respect, this is persuasion rather than inducement.

Inducement is a special case of exchange in which *a transfer of resources occurs.* As Cartwright (1965, p. 17) points out, "In some situations, the exercise of influence . . . involve[s] relinquishing ownership or control of a resource, as when money is paid for services. But it is possible to exert influence without giving up a resource, as illustrated by the sharing of information . . . " An inducement, as defined here, occurs

---

[4]A number of authors have used social exchange as a general approach to social organization and as a kind of metatheory. The discussion of inducements here touches on some of the ideas that are developed at length in Homans (1961), Thibaut and Kelley (1959), and Blau (1964).

only when there is the passing of control over some resource by the influencer either directly to an authority or to some broker in the transaction. Any "exchange" in which the influencer maintains control of the resource being used is defined here as persuasion.[5]

An inducement may be a payment for services already rendered or a deposit for future, unspecified actions. In other words, much inducement influence may involve a more generalized medium of *obligations* rather than the simple barter of resources for preferred outcomes. To illustrate, an influencer may give various inducements (for example, political support or campaign contributions) to an elected official. In return, he receives not some binding decision on a specific issue but a political I.O.U. This obligation which he gets in exchange for his inducements may be saved until an occasion arises for him to call for payment.

Just as an influencer may become a political creditor by virtue of past inducements provided, he can become a political debtor for past services rendered. At election time, he may be called on to fulfill his end of the bargain by providing the inducements owed. Many politicians are eager to create obligations to themselves by doing small favors for others; such obligations can be converted into specific inducements at election time or when a crisis occurs.

Inducements are, like constraints, typically implicit. Mitchell writes

An implicit bargain is one in which the conditions of agreement are not spelled out. . . . Usually, one party is expected to do something to which the other party is expected to reciprocate at some eventual time; but this is not always guaranteed. . . . A politician will vote for a measure to please another politician with the hope that eventually the latter will repay the assumed obligation (Mitchell, 1962, p. 295).

Such bargains run the risk that the terms will not be identically understood by both parties in the transaction; the size of the obligation that one party feels he owes may not be as

---

[5]This excludes the broken promise or the bluff which is discussed below.

large as that which the other feels is owed him. But such dis-
agreements over price clearly suggest the recognition by both
parties that some sort of *quid pro quo* is involved in their
transaction; the fairness of the terms, not the existence of the
transaction, is called into question.

The points made above on the wording and authorship of
constraints apply equally to inducements. A congressman,
who had not expected a campaign contribution from a particular constituent might be told by this would-be influencer
that, if he votes for proposal X, he will *not* get a substantial
contribution. Such an influence attempt is not a threat but a
rather ambiguous and implicit promise which the congressman would be advised to have clarified. Any negatively worded
offer *not* to add some new *advantage* is an implicit inducement, not a threat. As before, the influencer must be the
author, not simply the reporter of advantages, or else we are
dealing with persuasion rather than inducements.

The advantage need not be made conditional on the desired
action. An influencer might make a large campaign contribution to force an obligation. Or a partisan group which owned
land that it wished to have the city develop as a public recrea-
tion area, might donate the land to the city in the hope that
the diminished public cost might make its development more
attractive to the city.

C. Persuasion. Persuasion involves some change in the
minds of the authorities without adding anything new to their
situation. It involves making them prefer the same outcomes
that the influencer prefers.

Persuasion may be based on the convicition that the influencer's argument is correct. Such a conviction may in turn be
based either on the content of the argument that is made or
on the belief in the expertness of the influencer without any
clear understanding of the arguments given. Persuasion influence may also occur without the conviction that the influencer is right. It may be based simply on the intrinsic grati-
fication that comes from pleasing the influencer or refrain-
ing from displeasing him. If one of my goals is my friend's

happiness, then my orientation toward alternative X will be changed if I discover that this alternative will affect his happiness. His attitude is new information for me which changes my original conception of the effects of the alternative on my own goals.

Approval and disapproval as a means of influence are very interesting in this regard. Approval may be influential for two reasons: (1) it may be regarded by the recipient as an implicit promise of future rewards. Thus, he may vote to please his boss on the expectation that this pleasure will be translated into more tangible rewards when promotions and salary raises are being considered; or (2) the influencer's approval may be intrinsically rewarding. He may be a friend whose pleasure in the outcome of the decision is its own reward. In this case, there is no expectation of getting future benefits except those that stem from the relationship itself. The first of these examples represents inducement influence while the second involves persuasion. Similarly, disapproval may be either an implicit threat of future disadvantages or it may be psychologically punishing. If it is the latter, it is persuasion rather than constraint.

Since the word persuasion usually has a more limited meaning than the variegated one given here, it is worth underlining this category with a number of examples. If the brother of a member of a city council asks him to vote against a proposed fluoridation ordinance because he finds it objectionable, the councilman may do so even if he, personally, has nothing against fluoridation. The brother *may* give no reasons why he considers it objectionable and make no effort to convince the councilman of its undesirable characteristics. Or, the health officer may come to the council meeting and give arguments in favor of fluoridation which are not understood by the councilmen but which, on the basis of their faith in his expertness, convince the council to pass fluoridation. Finally, the health officer may present the council with a detailed description of the experiments conducted and the exhaustive checks made by scientists on possible dangers in such a way that the councilmen are left with a deep conviction of the desirability of fluoridation. Each of these is an example of persuasion.

Persuasion influence is not always distinguished from constraint and inducement influence by the degree of coerciveness involved. Any means of influence may vary in (*a*) the amount of restriction it places on the behavior of the targets and (*b*) on the degree of bindingness it carries for them.

a) On the amount of restriction, imagine that a school board is threatened with punishment if they pick site X for a school, but are left free to pick any other site. Alternatively, by an overwhelming propaganda campaign replete with lies, the school board might be manipulated into seeing compelling and overriding advantages in site X which do not exist. They may be less "free" to consider alternative sites in such circumstances than they are under the influence of threats.

b) A similar point can be made for degree of bindingness. If by completely binding influence, we mean a change in probability such that $P_a = 1.0$, force or the threat of force is not necessarily more binding than persuasion. The prospect of a possible punch in the nose may not completely deter someone from choosing an undesired alternative when the "persuasive" orders of a hypnotist leave him no choice. Manipulation, lying, hypnosis, "hidden" persuasion, "brainwashing," advertising, propaganda, are all names for particular kinds of persuasion influence, as long as they involve the manipulation of the target's orientation rather than the addition of sanctions to the situation. There is no implicit hierarchy of morality involved in the classification of means of influence.

Scope and site of influence

There has been a healthy emphasis among students of power on the necessity of specifying the areas over which influence extends. This emphasis comes from a reaction against a view of power relations as one of dominance-submission. Clearly, the influence relation being discussed here is not a general relation of dominance and subordination. Yesterday's partisan is today's authority and vice versa. Influence has already been narrowed in scope by making it refer only to certain specified actions of authorities, those which affect the probability of accepting preferred alternatives.

There is, however, a sense in which influence can be regarded as "content free" or independent of the subject matter of the decision. If a set of would-be influencers unequivocally control some resource, then they have a basis of influence which is not altered when the decision shifts from urban renewal to schools to fluoridation. A resource is still a resource and is unaltered by changes in the content of the decision as long as the authorities remain constant.

However, a resource for one set of authorities may not hold for another set. This suggests that the crucial aspect of the scope of influence is not the content of the decision but the *arenas* or *sites* in which resources are relevant. "The *arena* of power," write Lasswell and Kaplan (1950, p. 78) "is the situation comprised by those who demand power or who are within the domain of power." Similarly, Dahl (1966, p. 338) suggests that the "situation or circumstances in which an opposition employs its resources to bring about a change might be called a *site* for encounters between opposition and government." The site of an influence attempt can be identified with the target of influence; each set of authorities represents a different site.

Scope of influence, I am suggesting, should refer to the sites of influence rather than the content of issues. Thus, a given partisan group might be capable of exercising great influence over the President's decision to introduce a bill into Congress. On the very same issue, it might have little capability of exercising influence over a congressional committee which is considering the bill.

The assertion that resources are content-free with respect to any given site needs an important qualification. It is true only if the *control* of these resources is unaffected by the content of the decision. Many resources depend on the ability of the influencer to control the actions of other people. A union leader, for example, who holds the threat of a strike as a major resource in bargaining cannot call a strike on any issue at any time. The existence of this resource is very much dependent on the content of the issue. If it concerns a matter of fundamental union concern, then his ability to add the disadvantage of a strike is unquestionable; if he attempts to apply this resource in areas that are peripheral or irrelevant to his followers, his resource may be quite questionable. At the very least, to institute a strike in the latter case will require that he use additional resources to influence his membership that would not be required in the first case. If one cannot assume a constancy of control over resources regardless of the issue, then it is necessary to specify the scope of resources not only by indicating the applicable authorities but also by indicating the range of applicable decisions. Note, however, that the designation of scope would not consist of an *ad hoc* classification of content such as "economic" issues, "education" issues, and "political" issues, but would clearly focus on the relation of the issue to the influencer's control of resources.

Cost of influence — Use cost in M

There are a number of possible concepts of the "cost" of influence. A very important one considers the sacrifices that a would-be influencer must make in exercising influence and, in particular, the alternative use of his resources which he foregoes. However, this concept of "opportunity costs" is different from the one used here which focuses on the resources consumed in the influence transaction. These transactional costs include the resources involved in communicating and completing an act of influence and in maintaining an organization for such purposes.

There are a wide variety of specific resources which can be used to bring about influence. It is helpful to think of costs as involving the generalized inducement resources described above as *obligations.* Carrying out influence involves making commitments which place a future call on one's resources. The transactional cost of influence is the cost of fulfilling obligations contracted.

Fixed costs and variable costs. Partisan groups which participate regularly in the arena of politics generally find it necessary to maintain their resources in a state of high liquidity or readiness. To be able to influence when the occasion arises, one must spend resources to maintain readiness. Such costs transcend any particular act of influence; they represent an overhead cost which can be distributed over a series of acts. The cost of maintaining a defense establishment to be used as a constraint in international politics is an example of such fixed costs. The cost of employing a public relations firm to enhance reputation is another example. The expenses of a legislative representative or lobbyist by an organization interested in influencing Congress is still another example of a cost of influence which, while not specific to any single influence attempt, may be an important part of the total cost of influence for a partisan group.

Besides such relatively fixed costs, the sheer act of bringing influence to bear on the authorities will involve some cost. If we are concerned with persuasion influence, then the costs involved are the resources consumed in changing the orientation of the authorities. Included in such campaign costs are any which were preparatory to the act of attempted persuasion. For example, the costs to a group of professors who wished to encourage Congress to support a disarmament treaty would include not only the resources used to wire congressmen and the expense of a full page advertisement presenting their views in the *New York Times* but those used to solicit signatures for the advertisement and to establish contact with supporters around the country and enlist their participation.

Research costs are included here as well. A local group which wishes to have the community approve money for a new high school might have to spend considerable resources acquiring information which would enable them to answer arguments which are or might be raised. Having acquired such information, they might then have additional expenditures in getting this information to the voters. Both types of expenditure would be included as part of the cost of influence.

In some instances, a group which was involved in an effort at persuasion might solicit funds from supporters at the same time they were attempting influence. For example, an organization might mail a message which presents an argument for the need for a new high school while in the same message they ask for donations to cover the expenses of such a campaign. Suppose that the organization succeeds in raising sufficient money to offset the costs of the campaign. Would we then wish to say that the campaign had been costless? No, because the fact that money was raised at the same time that an influence attempt was taking place rather than before or after is fortuitous. The costs are there even if as a result of the influence attempt the solvency of the organization is greatly increased. An advertisement which costs a manufacturer $5,000 still has cost him $5,000 even if he shows a subsequent profit through the additional sales which his advertisement produces.

Inducements and constraints also must be communicated if the advantage or disadvantage being added is conditional on the behavior of the authorities. The costs of such communication may be trivial, as in the situation in which an influencer simply informs an official whom he has encountered what he will do if the official acts in the desired fashion. On the other hand, bargaining may be a long drawn-out process in which both parties must maintain a staff for the purpose of communicating promises or threats to the other side.

However, there is an additional element of cost for inducements and constraints which is not present for persuasion—the cost of changing the situation. Such situational costs are *noncontingent*, i.e., they are not affected by the outcome of the decision. The influencer might well show an increment in total resources or a net loss but, in either case, the resource cost to the influencer is the same. To make this point clear, it is best to consider separately the resources involved in constraints, inducements, and persuasion.

1. Inducements.   Any resource which is used to create new advantages for authorities is an inducement. For example, an influencer might offer money, opportunities, services, his vote on some future decision in which the influence roles are reversed, or many other things. In every instance, however, the carrying out of the inducement offered must involve the passing of control of the resource from the influencer. Thus, the influencer would have that much less money, opportunities to offer or freedom of action on future decisions as a result of the control over these which he has relinquished.

An inducer might make his offer conditional on the outcome of the decision. A candidate might, for example, promise the chairman of a large delegation to a nominating convention, an important post which the candidate would control only if he is subsequently nominated and elected. Consider the cost under each of three possible situations: (*a*) the delegation chairman refuses the offer; (*b*) the delegation chairman accepts the offer but the candidate is nevertheless unsuccessful; (*c*) the delegation chairman accepts the offer and the candidate is elected.

In the first of these situations, there is no resource cost since no influence occurred. In the second situation, we might also be tempted to say that there had been no cost since the contract was conditional on an event which never occurred. However, if we define the passing of control of resources as their commitment in such a way that they cannot simultaneously be committed elsewhere, then control over the important post has been relinquished or spent by the candidate regardless of what happens in the election.[6] Costs are incurred at the time of the influence attempt *when they are committed* rather than at the time of decision or later when they may be delivered. By this definition then, the cost in situation (*b*) and (*c*) above is identical despite the fact that the bargain must be fulfilled in one case and not in the other. In both cases, the post is committed by the influencer and he cannot use it again

---

[6]This formulation was suggested to the author by H. Andrew Michener.

without running the risk of having to default on his contract. Of course, the value to the delegation chairman of such a promise will vary depending on his estimate of the likelihood that the candidate will be successful, but the cost to the candidate is the same.

2. Constraints. Any resource which is used to create new disadvantages in the situation is a constraint. The carrying out of such influence involves committing resources in specified ways; the constrainer in doing so relinquishes control of the use of these resources. He may, of course, only threaten disadvantages which are conditional on the performance or nonperformance of certain acts. The candidate might, for example, threaten to campaign against the delegation chairman if the latter's support is not forthcoming. Again, we may consider some possibilities: (a) the chairman yields to the threat; or (b) the chairman ignores the threat and it is carried out. The cost is not contingent on whether the chairman yields to the threat; it is the same in both situations. The commitment to spend resources is made at the time of influence when the candidate binds himself to the costs of carrying out the threat. The resources in question are then no longer free for alternative uses.

One interesting implication of this definition of cost is that there is none at all beyond fixed costs and communication costs to the inducer or constrainer who is purely bluffing. Since the resources are not really being committed, nothing is being spent. However, the constrainer's credibility in future situations may be affected in ways that raise future costs. Similarly, an inducer who has no intention of fulfilling the contract he makes would have a situational cost of zero for the present decision but would undoubtedly have diminished credit on future decisions. This is equivalent to saying that it costs nothing if one writes a check with no funds to cover it; he has spent nothing at the moment, but there will be a future price to pay.

3. Persuasion. What are the situational costs of persuasion? There are three categories of persuasion resources:

(a) communication media and skills; *(b)* reputation for knowledge or wisdom; and *(c)* personal attraction. Communication media or skills are the basis for persuasion when authorities are convinced by the content of the argument. Reputation for knowledge is the basis of persuasion when the authorities believe the argument because of their faith in the expertness or intelligence of the influencer. Personal attraction is the basis for persuasion when authorities follow the desired course of action to please the influencer. This last involves accepting influence through what Kelman (1961) calls "identification" while the first two involve "internalization."

The resources involved in persuasion are not diminished by the act of influence—that is, *the situation cost is zero.* But, one might argue, surely one's reputation for wisdom might be diminished and the attraction one felt for him diminished by bad advice or misinformation which he might give. Yes, but his reputation might also be enhanced and the attraction for him increased by advice that turned out to be particularly good. In either case, the change in resources is not an intrinsic part of the act in question; such changes, like the credibility of threats or promises in future influence situations, must be dealt with under a different concept than costs. Fixed costs, communication costs, and situational costs are all independent of what contingencies occur. They are defined in such a way that they are the same regardless of the outcome of the decision; they are intrinsic to the influence transaction.

Other conceptions of cost

Profit and loss. A decision may have the effect of redistributing resources. If this is so, then there will be a change in the amount of resources which an influencer controls over and above the change from his commitment of resources in an act of influence. The result may be that he shows a net increment in resources or he may end up spending more than he receives back from the decision. A net increment is a profit;

a net decrement is a loss. This notion presupposes a concept of costs since it is defined as the difference between costs and returns from the decision. Net loss should not be confused with cost. A man who spends $1,000 to influence a decision and gets back $500 as a result of the outcome, has had a cost of $1,000, not $500.

Only resources and not all things of value to the influencer are being considered in the definition of costs and return. This means that there is no postulate that influencers will always seek a profit. When they are primarily seeking a profit, they are *investing* resources. When they are seeking some consummatory outcome, they are *spending* resources. One may seek prestige, honor, security and many other things besides resources.

Opportunity costs. Just as influencers seek to gain many things besides resources, they may give up other things besides resources in attempting influence. Thus, someone may be theoretically powerful because he controls many resources, but be unable to exercise influence because his resources are heavily committed and usable only at great sacrifice. As Harsanyi (1962, p. 69) observes, "if two individuals are in a position to exert the same influence over other individuals, but if one can achieve this influence only at the cost of great efforts and/or financial sacrifices, while the other can achieve it free of any such costs, we cannot say in any useful sense that their power is equally great." Similarly, Thibaut and Kelley (1959, p. 107) define a person's *usable* power as "the power that it is convenient and practicable for him to use. Power is not usable to the degree that its use penalizes the possessor. . . . " Deutsch makes the same point in adding to the definition of power, the

ability to act out a particular preference in behavior, or to reach a particular goal, *with the least loss of ability to choose a different behavior,* or to seek a different goal. Power in this extended sense is thus related not merely to the absence of imposed modification of behavior but also to economy of commitment, and to the capacity for alternative commitments in the future (Deutsch, 1966, p. 248).

The concept of opportunity costs has implications for how likely a potential partisan is to attempt influence. Any disadvantage to the influencer can be counted a cost in this sense and any advantage to him is a return or benefit. One can then predict that a rational potential partisan will attempt influence when his expected benefits outweigh his expected costs.

It is not clear that such a tautology is the most useful answer to the question of when a potential partisan will attempt influence. By limiting the definition of costs to the resources committed in an influence transaction, costs become only one among several factors determining influence attempts. Another variable, similar to a concept of usable power, is the amount of what Dahl (1961) calls the *slack resources* possessed by a group. In a pluralistic political system such as New Haven, he suggests, most groups possess resources which are not being used in political influence.

The amount of slack resources which a group has is a function of (1) the total amount they possess, and (2) the degree of commitment or liquidity of their resources. To the extent that they have little slack, their opportunity costs will be higher and they will be less likely to attempt influence. In short, the concept of opportunity costs points to important variables determining when influence will be exercised, but it seems preferable to limit the concept of costs to resources spent and to capture other disadvantages of exercising influence through other variables.

Future effects. The exercise of influence in a given situation may change the relationship between influencer and target in such a way that the costs of influence in future situations are raised or lowered. For example, a constrainer, by failing to carry out a threat, may reduce the credibility of his future threats. This will increase the future costs of such threats since, for a given amount of influence, either a more drastic threat will be required or else resources will have to be employed in raising the credibility. An inducer may fail to carry out a promised bargain thus reducing his credit in future transactions. This may require that he pay larger sums in the

future, or he may be required to pay at the time of the transaction, thus losing the advantages of credit and the flexibility
involved in making his advantages contingent on the authority's behavior. A persuader may lie or give bad advice with the
result that in the future his reputation for wisdom becomes
tarnished. A greater effort in communication may then be required for the same amount of influence.

Finally, the use of one means of influence may affect the
resources of another. An influencer who carries out a threat
may find that the target now has diminished affection. These
relational "costs" are a central focus of this book. They are
something to be explained and predicted rather than part of
the definition of costs. In short, the concept of costs here is
reserved for the commitment of resources while the other
possible "cost" phenomena enter in the various ways described
above.

5

Influence in repose

The question of who actually influenced the outcome of a decision should be kept conceptually distinct from the equally important question of who has the stable ability to influence the outcome. We usually want to do more than describe who has exercised influence in the past. Our knowledge of past influence can tell us something about who is likely to exercise influence in the future, but not everything. It is also important to know about potential influence.

Were there individuals or groups who *might* have influenced the outcome of past decisions under an appropriate set of conditions but did not exercise any influence? Some writers have suggested that such a question is scientifically meaningless. Polsby asks

How can one tell . . . whether or not an actor is powerful unless some sequence of events, competently observed, attests to his power? If these events take place, then the power of the actor is not "potential" but actual. If these events do not occur, then what grounds have we to suppose that the actor is powerful? (Polsby, 1963, p. 60.)

Clearly one must observe something about people who are alleged to have potential influence but this something need not be the exercise of influence. Imagine, for example, that we observed that all those who exercised influence possessed certain rare insignia but that some who possessed such insignia did not exercise influence. It would seem prudent under such circumstances to consider who possessed these insignia, their relationships to each other, and the conditions under which the bearers attempt influence.

It is a task for empirical research, and one with which this book is concerned, to specify when potential influence becomes actual influence. *Potential influence is synonymous with the control of resources.* Resources were defined above as some weight which, when properly applied in sufficient quantities, will change the probability of the outcome of a decision. Further, they must be controlled by the influencer and capable of being brought to bear on the authorities in interaction with them. This basis of influence will sustain the analysis of potential influence.

Degree of potential

Potential influence, like the rest of the power theme, has many ambiguities. In each of the following situations, the parties have potential influence: party leadership in the Senate with control over committee assignments; the President of the United States with his ability to make front page news when he wishes; the leader of a closely knit solidary group who commands the strong loyalty of the members; and the trusted elder statesman who has a reputation for prescience on public issues. The resources controlled here require little or no redeployment to be put to immediate use in the exercise of influence. They are already highly liquid and ready to be activated.

On the other hand, there may be another potential partisan, who has never taken much interest in politics. He may be a much admired figure with many things that could be turned into political resources if he were interested in doing so. However, to exercise influence, he would have to turn his attention from other things and deploy his resources in a new arena. He is not in the same state of readiness as the people in our previous example. Another similar case is that of a solidary group with little organization for collective action. The members are capable of exercising great influence but only if they can first pool their resources in some effective and organized way.

These examples suggest that we may distinguish resources from potential resources. Potential resources are resources of low liquidity, i.e., resources which can only be used to influence after they have been redeployed or mobilized in some fashion. Resources, without modifier, are resources of high liquidity, ready to be used for influence without extensive redeployment.

The distinction here, as in distinguishing the liquidity of economic assets, is not between sharp and discrete categories, but it is helpful in avoiding certain confusions in a concept of potential influence. There is clearly a distinction, for example, in the potential to carry out threats between a group which maintains an army for such purposes and one which merely possesses the abstract theoretical possibility of employing such an army. Thus, in international relations we recognize the difference between a country which has an existing ability to carry out a nuclear threat and one which has the potential to acquire such ability. In the former instance we would say that such a country had threat resources or threat potential; in the second case, we would say that they had the potential to acquire such a threat potential.

Amount of resources

It is of major importance for understanding potential influence to know not only the liquidity of resources but also their distribution among potential partisans. *The amount of resources that a unit possesses should not be confused with the amount of influence it has exercised.* There are many reasons why even one with an abundance of resources may not exercise influence on a given decision.

1. His resources may be limited in scope. He may be uncertain of his control, if he attempts to use his resources on a given issue. This is particularly true for those whose resources depend on the commitment of a constituency. The lower the trust which such a constituency invests in a leader, the more likely he is to refrain from attempting influence. The actions

of leaders in such situations are better understood as efforts
to convert potential resources into actual resources than as
influence attempts. Thus, a personal attack on public officials
might seem irrational if viewed as an attempt to exercise influence over them. But it appears quite rational if, through
personalizing an enemy, the energies of a group become mobilized for future influence. In contrast, a leader with the un-
conditional loyalty of his followers might refrain from using
his influence for one of the other reasons below but not because his resources are limited in scope.

2. He may care very little about the outcome of most
issues and thus have no motivation for influence despite his
ability. For most people, as Dahl points out, "Politics is a
sideshow in the great circus of life" (1961, p. 305). Or, as
Mitchell (1962, p. 97) puts it, "Men are not restlessly seeking
power in the polity, nor do those who have power . . . exercise
it to the fullest. Some citizens do not even perceive that they
possess power, and others shy away from it, for the costs of
acquiring and using it are deemed excessive."

3. He may have some preference on an issue but feel that
the transactional costs are greater than the gain he might get
from the outcome. Assuming that his resources are limited,
he will have to establish priorities and he may be forced to
ignore some issues in order to pursue others.

4. He may feel that his resources will be inadequate to
meet those that are countervailing. Existing competition may
raise the costs above the amount he is prepared to pay. Furthermore, he may choose not to use his resources for fear of
backlash. "A power-holder may prefer not to exercise all his
potential power for fear of inciting others into a struggle,"
Mitchell suggests (1962, p. 98).

For all these reasons, the absence of influence on a particular issue or set of issues cannot be taken as evidence against
the existence of potential influence. Nor does a defeat necessarily imply a lack of resources. It may also reflect a lack of
strong motivation. We would not say that a millionaire who
bid $50,000 for a painting was a pauper simply because a

poorer but more intense art lover bought the painting for $60,000.

Finally, resources may be used more or less skillfully. Some may lose because they spend resources inefficiently, wasting them and producing less effect on a decision than they might have had. "Skill in politics," Dahl points out (1961, p. 307), "is the ability to gain more influence than others, using the same resources." In sum, statements about a group's potential influence are statements about the amount of resources it controls and are not confirmed or disconfirmed simply by observing whether it was on the winning side on some set of past issues.

Slack resources

By itself, the distribution of resources in a system tells us very little about who will attempt influence. Presumably, it tells us something about how likely a group is to be successful once an attempt is underway, but even this is problematic. Depending on the competition, a very large or a very small amount of resources may be necessary to produce significant influence. Typically, the available resources which are actually used on any given decision are a tiny fraction of the total. "Very few people seem to exploit their resources to the limit in order to influence public officials; and even political officials often have resources available to them which they do not fully use" (Dahl, 1961).

There is nothing puzzling about the existence of such slack. Just as we would hardly expect shoppers in a department store to spend their life savings every time they went shopping, neither would we expect potential partisans to be so profligate in their use of resources. All influence has some transactional costs and there is no reason to think there are fewer political misers or, at least, prudent managers, than we find in the economic realm.

Even more important, there are many channels other than political ones by which individuals are able to satisfy their needs. Political resources may typically be utilized in other ways. As Dahl describes "homo civicus";

. . . the chances are very great that political activity will always seem rather remote from the main focus of his life. . . . Political action will seem considerably less efficient than working at his job, earning more money, taking out insurance, joining a club, planning a vacation, moving to another neighborhood or city, or coping with an uncertain future in manifold other ways (Dahl, 1961, p. 224).

To put it crudely, many an individual may prefer buying a new car to buying a councilman.

Mobilization of resources

The existence of slack resources in a group means untapped potential. A major problem for partisan groups is the mobilization of potential resources. This process is logically prior to the exercise of influence: one must have usable resources before entering the political fray. The history of many social movements is the history of "taking up the slack," the mobilization of resources followed by their exercise on numerous specific decisions.

Political actions must be judged not only in terms of their immediate influence—that is, their effect on the outcome of a specific decision—but by their creation of new resources as well. It is in this sense that an action such as the civil rights March on Washington in the summer of 1963 must be evaluated. It would be shortsighted (and quite possibly inaccurate as well) to argue that such a demonstration was a failure because it did not "change any votes" in Congress when in fact it may have had the effect of creating a continuing participation among thousands who had previously never taken part in the civil rights movement.

A number of political phenomena can only be understood in this light. The "Black Power" movement, for example, has been criticized for destroying a coalition between white liberals and Negroes, a coalition which has exercised considerable influence. By splitting this coalition and mobilizing its enemies, it is argued, the black power advocates weaken the civil rights movement. There is undoubtedly truth in this argument when judged from the standpoint of the coalition as a whole. But consider it from the standpoint of partisan leaders who wish to tap the potential resources in the urban ghettoes of the North and of poor Negro farmers in the South. The existing coalition did not mobilize such groups but their alienation and bitterness provides the basis for a potentially explosive mobilization. To focus these feelings on political objects is to create a readiness for political action which converts potential resources into actual ones. It remains to be seen whether organizations such as the Congress on Racial Equality (CORE), the Student Non-Violent Coordinating Committee (SNCC), and the Mississippi Freedom Democratic Party will be *successful* in mobilizing the support of their intended constituency. But their strategy must be understood in terms of this goal rather than evaluating success in terms of immediate influence.

A similar point can be made with respect to many community organization efforts in urban areas. Organizing attempts associated with or influenced by veteran community organizer Saul Alinsky frequently follow tactics which emphasize creating sharp confrontations with public officials and efforts to surprise and embarrass such officials. The use of such constraints and the threat of their use may produce some immediate impact on decisions but even when there is no tangible influence, the group may regard a particular incident as a success. Members will point to the newspaper publicity which the group received and the increased awareness of its existence in the community. If "success" is judged in terms of immediate influence, such claims might appear to rely on a false coin—a confusion of public attention with actual influence on policy. However, if success is judged in terms of building organizational support and tapping potential resources, the coin *may* be quite real. Whether such tactics actually lead to increased support for the organization is an empirical question. My point is not that they are desirable and necessarily successful tactics but that their success must be judged by the criterion of mobilizing slack resources.

TYPES OF RESOURCES

All resources do not have identical importance for the stability of influence. Some may be highly specific and particularistic in scope. A congressman's wife, by her control over the giving or withholding of affection, possesses a resource which can be used to influence her husband's vote on bills before congress. However, such a resource grows out of her particular relationship to the congressman and does not extend to those with whom she has no special relationship.

There are certain resources which are both of high applicability across a variety of authorities and of high stability of value over time within a particular set of authorities. The possession of such general resources rather than of more idiosyncratic ones is of significance for understanding the stable potential to influence the outcome of decisions.

Resources can be distinguished according to their means of utilization. A resource which can be used to threaten disadvantages will not necessarily serve as a resource for persuasion. Thus, we consider each means in turn.

Constraint resources

An individual or group may be said to have constraint resources if they can add some new disadvantage to the situation of some specified set of authorities. Some constraint resources are extremely specific in their range of applicability. For example, a blackmailer may have damaging information which he can use to threaten a single person; it would not serve to create disadvantages for anyone else. On the other hand, there are constraint resources of such generality that no individual is immune. Violence, for example, is such a resource.

The content of constraint resources depends on the nature of the social system one is studying. The threat of assasination, physical abuse, or the seizure of persons and property by force, are not equally important within a relatively integrated country such as Sweden and a sharply divided one such as South Vietnam. As we approach more normatively integrated forms of social organization, the content of constraint resources changes. The threat of violence becomes less important than the threat of denunciation. The withdrawal (or threatened withdrawal) of political support and the destruction (or threatened destruction) of public esteem become the significant constraints. The withdrawal of support may be used by spokesmen for solidary groups against elected officials although there must be some initial degree of support before this could be considered a constraint, that is, there must be something to withdraw. The ability to destroy reputation is a more widely shared resource, although those who are themselves well respected seem to possess greater ability in this regard. Presumably, a denunciation of a Presidential candidate by the head of the Ku Klux Klan brings with it less damage to the victim's reputation than an identical denunciation by General Eisenhower.

Besides those who can withdraw political support and those who can damage reputation, anyone who possesses generalized inducement or persuasion resources can use these to constrain. For example, a man who is able to influence an important school board decision *for whatever reason* can threaten to use his resources against the mayor if the mayor does not in turn follow his wishes on some decision.

Inducement resources

Similar points apply here as well. Some things are inducements only to a very small number of people. Heroin, for example, is undoubtedly a powerful resource if the authorities happen to be drug addicts. Since few are, it has little generalized utility as a resource.

Money on the other hand, is of extreme generality as an inducement. It has important limitations however. They occur not because there are authorities who do not value money but because of social constraints which prohibit its use as a means of influence under many conditions. In many situations, the open use of money as an inducement is defined as bribery. While there may be some private use of such inducements, money generally must be converted to some form of legitimate inducement before it can be used as a resource.

For this reason, wealth per se can be considered more of a potential than an existing resource. Many wealthy people do, of course, have inducements since wealth is frequently associated with key institutional positions. A leading businessman in a community may have many resources which stem from his position on the board of the local bank, his affiliation with a number of different financial and industrial concerns, his critical position in several important voluntary associations, and so forth. A retiring elderly widow who is much richer may possess none of these positions; her wealth would not be deployed in such a way that it could be directly used to produce inducements for authorities.

Those who control resources of any variety may offer this control to others as an inducement. A person who holds a position in an elaborate network of institutional and interpersonal relationships possesses a powerful set of inducements. It is virtually certain that there will be some present or future alternative that he can influence and that the authorities will care about. Even if there is no present alternative under consideration, it is a valuable political asset for any interested party to have such an influential person obligated to him.

To have authority over any important area of decision implies the possession of stable inducement resources. If the mayor wishes to influence the head of the Urban Renewal Board, he is in a position to offer numerous inducements (or threaten numerous constraints). If there is some present decision which the Urban Renewal head cares about, an immediate transaction may be concluded. If there is not, the mayor can simply credit his account for future use.

Persuasion resources

To review the earlier discussion of persuasion resources, there are three types: *(a)* communication media and skills—

the basis for persuasion when authorities are convinced by information and the content of the argument; *(b)* reputation for wisdom—the basis for persuasion when authorities are convinced by their faith in the influencer; and *(c)* personal attraction—the basis for persuasion when authorities follow the desired course of action to please the influencer. Some persuasion resources are highly limited in scope. Personal attraction is only a resource for those who know and like the would-be influencer; expertness is only a resource in those areas in which the influencer is considered knowledgeable. Are there more generalized and stable persuasion resources?

Each of the above bases of persuasion can be general as well as specific. A person who occupies a key "gatekeeper" position in the flow of communication has an important general persuasion resource. Schramm writes

At every point along the [communication] chain, someone has the right to say whether the message shall be received and retransmitted, and whether it shall be retransmitted in the same form or with changes. In other words, all along the chain are a series of *gatekeepers,* who have the right to open or close the gate to any message that comes along. (Schramm, 1963, p. 176).

Such gatekeepers control the definition of an issue in important ways and this can be an extremely important source of influence. Indeed, Schattschneider argues (1960, p. 68) that "the definition of the alternatives is the supreme instrument of power; the antagonists can rarely agree on what the issues are because power is involved in the definition."

The control of gatekeeping functions is not the only general persuasion resource. Skill in writing and speaking may transcend a given issue or set of authorities. Personal attraction can also be generalized to some degree. Charm and charisma can be cultivated so that they cover many authorities and, thus, qualify as a general basis of persuasion.

A particularly widespread general persuasion resource is *reputation.* There are individuals who are respected not because of any *specific* knowledge they may have on the issue at hand but because they are believed to be generally "sensible," "sound," "reliable," "unselfish," "intelligent," and so forth. In other words, they are believed to possess certain stable personal qualities that transcend any given issue and make their opinion more convincing. A highly successful military commander, for example, may find that his success is regarded by voters as a sign of grace. While his persuasion resources on issues involving military matters may be particularly great, he will carry with him a generalized reputation which acts as a resource—even on issues for which he has no special qualifications.

There are many things which contribute to the acquisition of reputation. In one society, it may be purity of behavior and asceticism while in another it may be worldly success. Personal characteristics play an important role in the control of such persuasion resources. A public display of foolishness or the disclosure of some private immorality may destroy such resources even though the behavior involved has no relevance for the matters on which the persuader may subsequently express judgment.

The argument that reputation is a resource has implications for the "reputational method" of studying power. A number of investigators interested in the operation of power in the community have elicited lists of names of community "leaders." Typically, a panel composed of heads of civic associations or some other group actively involved in public affairs is asked to nominate individuals and the nominees are in turn interviewed.

This method of studying community power has been sharply attacked both for the interpretations that are made of the list of names obtained and, in more basic ways, for the use of such questions at all.[1] To quote Polsby (1963, p. 51), "asking about reputations is asking, at a remove, about behavior. It can be argued that the researcher should make it his business to study behavior directly rather than depend on the opinions of second hand sources."

---

[1]For a critical review of the use of this method in community studies, see Polsby (1963), especially pp. 45-68; and Wolfinger (1960).

But if reputation is a resource, there is a theoretical justification for studying reputational leaders: one is concerned with them because their reputation is a form of potential influence. W. Gamson (1966b, p. 124) suggests operationalizing such reputation at the community level by asking a relevant set of authorities the following question: "In many communities, there are people who are generally listened to when they take a position on community issues because they are believed to have good judgment. Are there any such people in _____?" The validity of such a question concerns how well it measures reputation, not its connection with influence behavior.

Those who are named as "reputational leaders" simply comprise a pool of individuals with resources. No claim is made that they form a ruling elite or even a cohesive group of any sort; such claims must rest on demonstration of a number of additional characteristics. Those with resources may or may not be friendly with each other socially. If they all belong to the same clubs and organizations, this is an important additional fact about the organization of resources in the community. . . . Similarly, agreement on policy among reputational leaders is an empirical question. . . . The only thing we wish to maintain about the list of reputational leaders is that, because they possess significant amounts of resources, their social organization is significant for the understanding of stable power relations in the community (W. Gamson, 1966b, p. 124).

In the particular sample of 18 New England communities that were studied, reputational leaders were frequently active but on opposite sides of an issue. When active and united, they do appear to influence the outcome of community issues. This indicates that they possess *some* resources and the argument here suggests that one such resource is their reputation itself.

SUMMARY — *use this as part of your summary*

The discussion of influence in the past two chapters has involved many byways. It is worth collecting the major arguments at this point for some overview. A partisan group can be said to have exercised influence if and only if there is a difference between two probabilities, P_a and P_b. P_b is the probability that a preferred outcome will occur if the partisan group can or will take no action contingent on what the authorities propose to do. P_a is the net result of the addition of the potential partisan group to the situation.

Influence can be operationalized in three ways. First, one may restrict statements about the influence of a group to the increase in the relative frequency of success when the group works for issues over the frequency of success when they oppose them. Second, one may measure influence by shift in subjective probability. If a set of informed observers would consider the preferred alternative a better bet after a partisan group has made its stand known and worked for it, then the group can be said to have exercised influence. Finally, one can approach the exercise of influence indirectly, examining the occurrence of influence attempts and observing the resources possessed by those who make such attempts.

A group may exercise negative influence through creating resistance on the part of authorities or through activating backlash. The amount of influence is the degree of probability shift in the intended direction and if the probability of success after influence is lower than the initial probability, then negative influence has been exercised.

The basis of influence refers to resources that, when applied to authorities, change the probability of the outcome of a decision. A resource must be controlled by the influencer and capable of being brought to bear on authorities in interaction with them. The means of influence refers to the manner in which the influencer uses such resources. Constraint influence is the addition of new disadvantages to the situation or the threat to do so, regardless of the particular resources used. Inducements are the addition of new advantages to the situation or the promise to do so. Persuasion involves some change in the minds of the authorities without adding anything new to their situation.

It is desirable to specify the areas over which resources are applicable and, hence, over which influence can be exercised.

Since resources are defined in terms of sets of authorities, it is better to talk about the scope of influence in terms of relevant *sites* rather than the type of issue covered. However, to the extent that control of resources is problematic and dependent on the content of the issues on which it is exercised, issue content may also be a relevant aspect of scope.

There are a number of different phenomena that are sometimes covered under the concept of costs of influence, but it is used here to refer to the resources committed in the influence transaction. Included in such transactional costs are the resources used to maintain an organization and state of readiness to influence, the resources involved in communicating the act of influence to the target, and the resources used in changing the situation of the target. These can be defined in such a way that they are intrinsic to the influence transaction and not contingent on the outcome of the decision. The alternative concept of "opportunity costs" points to important variables that are handled here by the total amount of resources possessed and the liquidity of such resources.

Who has actually influenced decisions and who can influence decisions are independent questions. The first refers to changes in the probability of decision outcomes; the second refers to the possession of resources. Potential resources should be distinguished from actual resources. The former are resources of low liquidity, that is, resources which can only be used to influence after they have been redeployed or mobilized in some fashion.

The amount of resources that a unit possesses is not the same as the amount of influence it has exercised. Groups may possess resources and still not exercise influence for many reasons. These include limitations on the scope of resources, a lack of motivation or concern about the issue, a high commitment of existing resources which forces the establishment of priorities, and an amount of competition that makes costs out of line with the importance of the decision.

In most political systems, there are large amounts of resources which are not in use at any given moment. The existence of such slack resources has two important implications for potential partisans. First, it means that in many cases, a very small amount of resources will be necessary to exercise influence. Second, such slack also means the existence of untapped potential. The mobilization of this potential will frequently dominate the strategy and tactics of disaffected groups and their actions can best be understood as efforts at the generation of resources rather than the exercise of influence.

Resources which are applicable over a variety of authorities and which are stable over time are particularly significant for understanding potential influence. Constraint resources tend to be more important in less-integrated systems. However, the withdrawal of political support and the discrediting of reputation are important constraint resources even in relatively integrated systems. A person who holds a key position in an elaborate network of institutional and interpersonal relationships has an important set of general inducements to offer.

General persuasion resources include communication gatekeeping and skill in presentation, reputation, and personal attraction. Reputation is particularly important as a generalized resource. It becomes important to identify those who possess it not because such people are a ruling elite or a group which has necessarily exercised influence but because their reputation is a resource and, hence, they have potential influence.

The zero-sum issue

Various issues which arise in discussions of the power theme should now be more easily handled. One of these concerns the question of whether power is usefully viewed as something which one party exercises over another or as the capacity of one party to achieve its goals. This has been formulated as the "zero-sum" issue. A zero-sum or, more accurately, constant sum conception of power assumes that power has the following property: that being fixed in overall quantity, any gain to one unit must imply a loss to another unit. Thus, if some have more power, others must have less.

First, one might take it as a statement of the exercise of influence. It would seem to be undeniable that there are built-in limits on the extent to which influence can occur. If a group favoring an alternative has changed the probability of its being accepted by a given amount, those opposed have been set back by the same amount. Power is, indeed, "zero-sum" in this sense.

However, a more meaningful statement of the issue centers around the concept of resources. The statement above can be interpreted as the proposition that the more resources one group has, the less others will have. Under certain specified conditions, the resources are clearly fixed. If a decision does nothing other than allocate or redistribute existing resources, then the more that one group gains in such a redistribution, the more some other group will lose. If the decision, for example, involves the distribution of party offices between two rival factions in the party, it makes sense to think of the total resources being distributed as constant.

However, as Parsons and others argue, resources may be generated by decisions as well as distributed. Groups can, by depositing resources with a set of leaders whom they trust, find that they are better able to realize their goals than they could by using these resources to exercise influence themselves. In this sense, those who control these resources for a constituency and utilize them in their interests cannot be said to exercise power "over" them.

It is possible that those with more resources hold these resources in trust and exercise them effectively on behalf of those who have trusted them; or they may have conflicts of interest with groups without resources and use their resources to win relative advantage. The purpose to which influence is put brings us to the discontent theme.

6

The management of discontent

In exploring influence, we have taken the perspective of potential partisans affecting the choices of authorities. From the standpoint of authorities, another set of questions emerges. By their very nature, many choices will affect potential partisan groups in different ways. Authorities will inevitably satisfy some groups more than others. Only rarely will their choices be free of some element of conflict, that is, only rarely will there exist an alternative that is the first choice of all groups. This basic fact of conflict confronts authorities with the problem of managing discontent and containing influence.

From their perspective, the basic question is "how does one prevent those potential partisans who are injured or neglected by political decisions from trying to change the nature of the decisions, the authorities, or the political system within which decisions are made?" Authorities, I assume, wish to remain free from the pressure of external limits, free of influence attempts which more or less successfully tie their hands. If this sounds cynical, it need not be. For example, Arthur M. Schlesinger, Jr., (1965, p. 120) writes of the interregnum period following Kennedy's election as a test of the President-elect's "executive instincts and, in particular, of his skill in defending his personal authority against people striving, always for the best of motives, to contract his scope for choice."

The authorities in question may be operating to the best of their ability to satisfy the needs of as many potential partisans as possible. They may operate as justly as they possibly

111

can in situations involving conflicts of interest. They may conscientiously seek information from potential partisans so that they can meet these objectives. But, in the end, such authorities no less than self-interested or tyrannical ones, experience attempts to influence them as a limitation on their freedom of action. There are exceptions to this generalization—for example, in situations in which authorities may wish to stimulate pressure from one source to free themselves from some opposing source. But even this exception is governed by the desire to contain influence and thus remain free of its limits.

Perhaps it would be more accurate to say that authorities *qua* authorities desire limitations on the ability of potential partisans to exercise influence. Individuals occupying positions of authority may frequently desire great personal discretion in how they may use this authority because such discretion allows them to use their authority as a resource. Even if such discretion invites influence from others, at the same time it enhances their ability to influence others. Thus, those in authority may welcome freedom from public surveillance and accountability which act as control devices on both potential partisans and themselves. Such desires are an outgrowth of their potential partisan role, not their authority role. From the standpoint of that collectivity for which they serve as agent, the increased opportunity for influence creates control problems; there is less guarantee in such situations that those with authority will function as agents instead of as independent operators. The demands of flexibility and adequate task performance may require that authorities be given some leeway, but the more that considerations of control are relevant, the more such leeway will be reduced.

RESPONSES TO INFLUENCE PRESSURE

Potential partisans who are discontented with the choices of authorities must be handled in some fashion. The most basic distinction in how such discontent may be handled is between some modification of the content of the decision and some effort to control the potential partisan. The former response deals with the object of discontent by modifying the outcome in some way; the latter deals with the source of the pressure. These responses to discontent have something in common.[1] Both aim at removing the pressure that potential partisans are likely to put on authorities, one by yielding ground and the other by directing counterinfluence.

Why call such counterinfluence social control instead of simply encompassing it under the previous discussion of influence? The answer is that the agents of such counterinfluence are acting *as agents of the social system.* We separate their actions in such a role from their actions in pursuit of personal values and interests in which they may use resources to affect the decisions of others. When they act upon potential partisans in some manner to prevent or lessen the likelihood of influence over an area in which they make binding decisions, they are acting in the role of authorities.

Altering the outcome of decisions

The distinction has been made between the efficiency of the political system in achieving collective goals and its bias in handling conflicts of interest. Potential partisans may be unhappy on either account. Those who are dissatisfied with the efficiency of the system feel that more effective leadership or institutions are needed. Government may be criticized as "wasteful" or "inefficient." Such dissatisfaction assumes a basic consensus within which decisions are made.

Discontent about the equity of the political system is more difficult to deal with because conflict is inherent in the nature of some decisions. It is impossible in such cases, even if they have some collective aspects, to meet the desires and interests of all potential partisans. When the problem is one of ineffective leadership on collective goals, then by "wiser" or "better"

---

[1] This argument is developed in Z. Gamson (1964).

choices, the discontent of potential partisans can be assuaged. When it involves the handling of conflicts, such notions as "better" invariably raise the question, "better for whom?"

Altering the outcome of decisions is one approach to the problem of discontent. The collective aspects of decisions present few problems for authorities that cannot be met by simply choosing different alternatives. As members of the same collectivity as the partisans, the authorities will presumably be easily susceptible to persuasion or education since the partisans and the authorities will benefit by the same alternative.

Discontent over the handling of conflict can also be treated by outcome modification although this has the effect of redistributing discontent rather than alleviating it. Nevertheless, there may be many reasons why authorities would prefer to see some groups more contented than others. They may share the values and interests of one group and prefer to satisfy them for that reason. Or, some may have more resources or access than others and they may relieve pressure by yielding ground to the most powerful among the potential partisans. *The greater the inverse relation between the amount of resources controlled and the amount of discontent among potential partisans, the freer the authorities are from influence.* In short, they are most free when those with the most discontent have the least ability to influence. To contain influence, outcome modification will move in this direction.

Finally, outcome modification may be a way of undercutting the mobilization of a partisan group which is in the process of converting dissatisfaction into a force for influence. By giving a little at the right time, authorities may prevent later, more important outcome modifications. "An astute set of authorities," Easton (1965, p. 408) suggests, "in Machiavellian fashion, often meets just enough [demands], at least so as to still any critical accumulation of discontent. In the language of practical politics, this involves offering sops or conciliatory outputs at just the right moment to head off any brewing storm of dissatisfactions." Social movements may falter on partial success, winning small victories which, while leaving basic dissatisfactions untouched, hamper the members in their ability to mobilize resources for further influence.

Social control

The alternative to outcome modification is social control. If such control is successful, then there will be little influence and, hence, no need for outcome modification. The authorities will maximize their room for maneuverability and such maneuverability has three virtues.

1. It allows the incumbent authority to exercise his own personal preference. He is free to act as he pleases and to do what he thinks best, within the limits of his role but without the additional limits imposed by influence.

2. If he has no particular preferences, the freedom from influence on a given issue enables him to use his authority as a resource to influence other decisions on which he has a partisan interest. In other words, successful social control increases the resources of authorities by allowing them discretion in the areas in which they exercise authority; such freedom allows them to use their authority as an inducement or constraint on other authorities whom they would influence. They could not use their authority as a resource if their hands were tied by pressure from partisans just as they would be similarly hampered by structural limitations on their freedom to use their authority.

3. Effective social control increases slack resources. This means that influence is cheaper. "Slack resources provide the political entrepreneur with his dazzling opportunity, . . ." Dahl writes (1961, p. 309). He can influence at bargain rates when the competition has been removed by effective social control.

The tendency for outcome modification and social control to be competing alternatives is nicely illustrated in a study of the impact of students on the operation of an experimental college (Z. Gamson, 1966). Within the college, two faculty subdivisions existed with differing orientations toward students, described by the author as "utilitarian" and "normative." The utilitarian orientation emphasized cognitive effects on students, was less concerned about developing high student commitment to the college and encouraged faculty to maintain some distance from students. The normative orientation emphasized reaching students personally as well as intellectually, encouraged high student commitment and promoted close, egalitarian relationships with students. The author discovered an apparent paradox—those groups within the faculty with the most intense and diffuse concern with students were less responsive to particular student demands than those with a more specific and contractual relationship.

The paradox, of course, was only apparent. While each social control orientation had its own characteristic strains, for a variety of reasons the utilitarian orientation was less successful in forestalling pressures for modification of curriculum decisions. As a result, the pressures for change were greater and the resultant modifications were more frequent and radical in the division with the utilitarian orientation. The normative orientation, while it produced problems of a different sort, proved a stronger fortress against pressures for curriculum change. Thus, student influence was greater where student-faculty relationships were more distant because the closer relationship in one case produced more potent social control and less outcome modification.

TYPES OF SOCIAL CONTROL

There are three general ways in which authorities can contain the influence of potential partisans at its source. They can (1) regulate the access of potential partisans to resources and their ability to bring these resources to bear on decision makers, (2) they can affect the situation of potential partisans by making rewards or punishments contingent on attempts at influence, or (3) they can change the desire of potential partisans to influence by altering their attitudes toward political objects.

Insulation

An extremely important set of controls operates by giving potential partisans differential access to authorities and to positions which involve the control of resources that can be brought to bear on authorities. Such selectivity operates at two points—entry and exit.

Selective entry. Not all social organizations can control who is let in but many exercise considerable selectivity. A society cannot, of course, control the characteristics of the infants born into it—at least not until the Brave New World arrives. This absence of selectivity makes the control problems more severe than those encountered by an organization that can control entry.

However, most societies do exercise control over entry through immigration. Normally, they do not ask others for their tired and poor and huddled masses yearning to be free. Once the demand for large quantities of unskilled labor has been met, they are more likely to request doctors and engineers and huddled intellectuals yearning to be rich. Those who are presumed to offer particularly acute control problems are not welcomed. This includes both those who are likely to commit a variety of individual acts of deviance and those who are likely to organize themselves or others into groups that threaten the existing social order. Societies, like other forms of social organization, try to simplify their subsequent control problems by refusing entry to those elements most likely to aggravate such problems.

Most complex organizations are able to exercise some degree of selectivity in entry although there is wide variability in this regard. A corporation about to hire an executive is interested in a wide variety of characteristics not directly relevant to job performance. These other characteristics are frequently relevant to control problems. Those who are highly independent or erratic or in other ways seem likely to use the resources of their position in a free wheeling manner are generally regarded with caution. Of course, extraordinary ability or an extraordinary situation may convince an organization that it ought to take risks, but this does involve the assumption of greater problems of subsequent control. In short, I am not asserting that the reduction of control problems alone determines who will be allowed access to important positions, but such considerations are one factor and the problems are minimized by admitting only orthodox people.

Organizations which have little control over whom they let in are confronted with more control problems than those organizations which can select. Prisons, state mental hospitals, public schools and other organizations that have large numbers of their members determined for them by other organizations in their environment have control problems which private mental hospitals and private schools do not have. State universities should, by the same token, have greater control problems than private colleges which exercise high selectivity.

An important aspect of selective entry is *self-selection.* Many voluntary organizations reduce their control problems inadvertently by attracting as members those who will "fit well" and will offer few control problems and by repelling those who are likely to be discontented. In such cases, selective entry occurs not by the organization refusing admittance to potentially difficult individuals but by such individuals removing themselves by not seeking entry.

Self-selection is influenced by the organization's image. *An organization's efforts to project an image which will differentiate it from others can be viewed as a social control device.* The manipulation of organizational image has other purposes as well, the major one of which is to increase the organization's attractiveness, thereby increasing its ability to compete for desirable members, clients, or customers. But the effects of selectivity can be distinguished from the effects of increased attractiveness. In the latter case, we would expect there to be a tendency for members of *all* subgroups in the organization's environment to show approximately the same degree of increase in numbers seeking entry.[2]

However, if the image is serving a function of differentiation rather than increased attraction, this will not be so. Instead, the numbers seeking entry will increase in some groups while decreasing in others, i.e., while the organization is becoming more attractive to some, it is becoming less attractive to others. When an organization's image serves such a process of differentiation we may think of it as serving a social control function; it is increasing selective entry through a process of self-selection among potential members.

Entry is not an all or nothing state. Once in, members may have differential access to resources and communication opportunities. All members of the House of Representatives cannot be members of the Rules Committee or of other committees which command large amounts of resources. One may regard most social systems as possessing a series of entry points each of which offers control opportunities by denying further access to certain categories of potential partisans. In fact, if the population arriving at each gate were sufficiently endowed with the "right" kind of individuals and the process of selection were infallible and produced no errors, there would be no need for any other kind of control. Neither of the conditions above is usually met so that other forms of control must come into play.

Besides denying some potential partisans access to positions that control resources, they may also be denied access to resources in other ways. They may be prevented from acquiring sufficient skill and knowledge for access. Daniel Lerner, for example, describes the Ottoman Imperium as "not

----

[2]This does not imply that the organization is equally attractive to all subgroups but only that there is a relative increase in attractiveness across the board. For example, Eisenhower received a relatively high Republican voting percentage from *both* businessmen and workers but the absolute percentage of each group that voted for him was quite disparate.

merely a variety of illiterate populations but an antiliterate elite, who regulated the daily round of public life by maintaining exclusive control over key points of contact between individuals and their larger environment" (1958, p. 113). A communication system which carried the news orally from the Ottoman center to scattered villages served "as an administrative technique of social control, not as an instrument for shaping enlightened public opinion." Preventing the acquisition of communication skills in a population of potential partisans with serious discontent is an aid in controlling such a population. Keeping such a population physically separated so that no sense of common interest or solidarity can easily develop may also be regarded as a way of preventing potential partisans from organizing and mobilizing potential resources for influence.

Subsequently, the lack of requisite skill and training may serve to justify the denial of access should such disadvantaged groups press for it. Members of such a group might be advised that giving them access in the absence of "proper qualifications" constitutes preferential treatment. Thus, the selective entry may be justified on highly legitimate and widely accepted criteria and this control device may be preserved from becoming the target of pressure *itself.*

Selective exit. Most of the above discussion of selective entry is applicable to selective exit as well. There are some differences worth noting. While some social organizations have small control over whom they let in as members, all have means of removing access. Societies may imprison, exile, or put to death members that prove too troublesome to be handled by other control techniques. Even prisons and state mental hospitals isolate some members from the rest; public schools can expel hard-core control problem students.

There is probably some tendency for selectivity in entry and exit to be inversely correlated. *Those organizations which exercise a great deal of control at entry should be less likely to use expulsion as a control device than those organizations which have little control over who gets in.* If they use care in selection and a "low-risk" policy of entry, they can afford to be more lenient in subsequent actions, and should need to rely less on such drastic measures as expulsion. Those with little control at the point of entry are likely to have a higher frequency of difficult cases that cannot be handled by other control techniques.

Examples of insulation through exit devices are numerous and for the most part obvious. A particularly striking case occurred in the winter following the U.S. military intervention in the Dominican Republic. The provisional government, buffeted by the continuing struggle among powerful partisan groups, attempted to relieve the pressure by requesting the voluntary exile of a number of army officers who were leaders of these groups. The unusual and striking thing in this instance is that the officers were themselves rivals and political enemies; thus, the meaning of the act as an attempt to contain influence is unusually clear. More typically, such actions are aimed at removing influence from a particular source and are not as readily recognizable as an act of social control.

The removal of access as a social control device is not without its own set of problems. Goffman (1964) has helped call attention to the fact that the use of such devices generates its own necessity for control. The removal of access tends to be regarded by the individuals involved as a mark of failure or repression and is consequently resented. This resentment may lead to action on the part of the victim. In the confidence game example from which Goffman draws his terminology, the "mark" may decide to complain to the police or "squawk." In our more drab terminology, the person who has been removed from access may translate his resentment into influence unless it is dealt with in some way. The devices which a social system uses to help a victim accept his failure quietly are now generally called, following Goffman's provocative article, "cooling-out mechanisms." We should expect any organization which makes widespread use of the removal of access as a control device to employ such mechanisms. For example, the device of "kicking upstairs" involves the removal

from access to a position which commands significant resources while assuaging the resultant discontent by an accre-
tion in status. Compulsory retirement at a given age is another
device which removes access without creating the danger that
the victim will squawk. As with discrimination in entry, discrimination in exit is most effective when it can be accomplished using accepted, universalistic criteria.

Sanctions

Social organizations maintain systems of sanctions to reward the "responsible" and to punish the "irresponsible" or
"deviant." If these words carry with them the connotation of
desirability and undesirability, it is because we are accus-
tomed to assuming a social control perspective. Whether being responsible is desirable depends on the nature of the social organization to which one is being responsible. Adolph
Eichmann was clearly acting responsibly from the standpoint
of Hitler's Germany. There may be a conflict between loyalty
to one's friends, constituents, or one's personal values and
one's responsibility as agent of the social system. A person's
loyalties and convictions may impel him to use the resources
of his position in an attempt to bring about decisions that he
believes are desirable. But in using his authority as a resource,
an individual is acting in the role of potential partisan rather
than authority and issues of control are created thereby.

Sanctions will follow what is considered to be the misuse
of authority. The limits which these sanctions impose on
freedom of action may not be desired by those who exercise
authority for it places limits on their ability to influence.
Such sanctions act as a control on both potential partisans
and authorities who would be potential partisans at other
times. Thus, partisans are typically prevented from openly
bribing officials and penalties exist both for attempting and
for accepting such illicit influence. Specified channels for
"proper" influence are frequently provided—for example,
petitioning or testifying at open hearings. Such channels

contain a double restriction. On the one hand, they restrict the use of resources by potential partisans by subjecting their influence attempts to public surveillance and accountability. On the other hand, they restrict the opportunity of the target of influence to use his authority as a resource which he can exchange in some transaction with potential partisans. From the standpoint of both parties, ex parte presentations may be tempting, allowing as they do for the freer use of reciprocal influence. From a social control perspective, such off-the-record contacts between potential partisans and authorities offer less assurance that the latter are operating as agents of the social system rather than exercising personal influence.

The bestowal and withdrawal of effective authority is an important sanction. Losing effective authority over an area is a double loss: it means that the loser now must spend resources to influence decisions where formerly he could simply exercise authority. Moreover, he has lost an important resource which he previously was able to use in influencing the decisions of other authorities. He is, thus, put in a position in which he has both lost resources and at the same time needs them more. The threat of withdrawing effective authority is, for these reasons, an important form of control on the "abuse" of such authority.

Social structural and normative limits exist on every authority which circumscribe his ability to use his powers as a resource and, hence, operate as a social control. If the limits are sufficiently great and remove from him any discretion in how he may use his authority, then he has no resource at all stemming from his position. Usually, he is left some area of discretion bounded by some set of limits, the violation of which will result in sanctions. If selection mechanisms have failed to prevent an "irresponsible" person from gaining access to resources, sanctions are an additional control that may keep him in line. If he is unmoved by such sanctions, he may be removed from his position. Short of removal, there are a wide variety of sanctions available. One may be passed over for promotion, denied salary increases, given less helpful and prestigeful facilities, and so forth. Daily life can be made exceedingly unpleasant by the noncooperation of associates on whom one is dependent for the performance of one's job. And the threat that one will not be given any benefit of the doubt in the decisions of others can be a powerful deterrent.

Social control is *not* the only consideration in the distribution of inducements and constraints in a social system. Individuals may be rewarded for outstanding performance or for being the son of the company president; they may be punished for their religion or their incompetence. Control is simply one aspect and in many cases may be far from the dominant one. It should be emphasized that this discussion is not intended as a complete explanation of why individuals are given access to resources or are rewarded; rather, it is an attempt to describe the manner in which such things can be and are used for social control, in addition to whatever other uses they may have.

Promotion within an organization has elements of both insulation and sanctions. It is likely to mean some change in access to resources while at the same time it contains certain rewards. The distinction here is an analytic one which is difficult to make in practice. A man who has just been made president of a major corporation now has authority over areas which affect large numbers of people in important ways. Furthermore, he is likely to have wide latitude in the use of this authority. Thus he has gained access to important new resources. On the other hand, there are many things which are personally rewarding to him in the promotion—the greater status, the greater pay, the challenge and difficulty of the job, and the additional resources which he has gained. To the extent that control elements are relevant to his promotion, they operate in a dual fashion. Perhaps he is allowed access to the new resources because he appears more likely than someone else of equal ability and qualifications to act strictly as an agent of the organization. He is given the rewards of the new position because as vice president of the company he has, even at some personal sacrifice, demonstrated his willingness to act as agent of the organization. In this case, access and sanctions amount to essentially the same thing and the distinction is artificial; however, in many other cases, the two processes of control are quite separate and distinguishing them alerts one to different features of the organization.

Persuasion

Persuasion attempts to control the desire rather than the ability to influence. Potential partisans may be persuaded in a variety of ways either that their interest is well served by political decisions or, if not served on a particular occasion, that the procedures by which decisions are made serve their larger interest. Such persuasion may involve emphasizing the collective aspects of decisions, making those aspects which involve conflict appear less salient or important. Thus, potential partisans may be persuaded that the authorities are operating in the interests of the larger collectivity to which both parties belong even if some *relative* disadvantage is involved for their own subgroup. If potential partisans are convinced that the overall system of decision making is unbiased, they will be more willing to accept temporary setbacks in the belief that "things will even out in the long run."

There is an interesting variety of words used to describe this social control technique—some of them highly pejorative and others complimentary. The approving words include education, persuasion, therapy, rehabilitation, and, perhaps more neutrally, socialization. The disapproving words include indoctrination, manipulation, propaganda, and "brainwashing." The choice of words is merely a reflection of the speaker's attitude toward the social system and its agents. If one believes the authorities are faithful agents of a social system which is accorded legitimacy, then they are "socializing" potential partisans when they exercise social control. If one sides with the potential partisans and identifies with their grievances against the authorities, then this latter group is using "manipulation" as a form of control. The behavioral referent, of course, may be identical in both cases; the choice of word reflects two different perspectives on the same relation.

As in the earlier chapters on influence, the word persuasion is used in the broadest possible sense to include any technique which controls the orientation of the potential partisan *without* altering his situation by adding advantages or disadvantages. Some examples may help to make this breadth clear. The withholding of information from potential partisans about adverse effects of decisions is a use of persuasion as a means of social control. The withholding of information on fallout from atomic tests in Nevada during the period prior to the nuclear test-ban treaty was apparently done to avoid increasing public pressure for the cessation of such tests. Similarly, almost all social systems try to keep knowledge of their failures from circulating lest it generate pressure for change. Potential partisans who acquire such information (perhaps from allies among the authorities) publicize it for exactly the opposite reason—in the hope that it will mobilize their constituency to action. The selective withholding of information, then, is a technique of social control through persuasion.

Surrounding authorities with trappings of omniscience is another case of this control technique. If the authorities are viewed as distant, awe-inspiring figures possessed of tremendous intelligence and prescience plus access to privileged information that is essential for forming judgments, then the potential partisan may hesitate to challenge a decision even when he feels adversely affected by it.

There is, however, a contrasting technique which *minimizes* social distance between potential partisans and authorities. By personal contact and the "humanization" of authorities, potential partisans may be encouraged to identify with them; this identification, in turn, produces a trust which makes influence appear less necessary. If the people making the decisions are just like me, then I need not bother to influence them; they may be trusted to carry out my wishes in the absence of influence.

Judged strictly as a social control device, awe offers certain protections that the humanization of authority does not. Minimizing the distance between authorities and potential partisans may encourage the development of trust but it also tends to increase access and allow greater opportunities for influence. The control gained by reducing the desire for influence may be offset by the control lost in increasing the capability of influence. Oracular authorities offer no such danger and usually require a minimum of access.

Doing one's duty. A particularly important use of persuasion as a source of control involves the activation of commitments or obligations to the social system. Potential partisans can be persuaded to refrain from trying to change or subvert those decisions that have unpleasant consequences for them by convincing them that they have a "duty" to honor such decisions. The importance of legitimacy for a political system comes from its connection with this control technique. If legitimacy is high, then there is a high potential for activating commitments and other, more costly forms of control may be avoided. For example, if "patriotism" and "the duty to serve one's country" are sufficiently strong, then there is no need for conscription; a voluntary army can be counted on. However, if legitimacy is weak and alienation toward the political system is prevalent, then the call to duty may sound hollow.

Not everyone is as committed to duty as the young hero of *The Pirates of Penzance* who insists on fulfilling his obligation to the pirates to whom he was mistakenly bound in childhood in spite of his strenuous disapproval of their profession. Still, a wide variety of unpleasant commitments may be accepted with good grace when there is a surplus of political trust. A good illustration of the dependence on such trust may be found in the relatively sudden increase in opposition to the Selective Service System. Students who were able to reach graduate school were, for many years, given *de facto* exemptions from compulsory service. As long as American foreign policy was generally supported, the unequal sacrifices demanded from different groups in the society did not become an issue. However, with the erosion of confidence stemming from American policy in Vietnam, not only the bases of deferment but conscription itself has been seriously challenged. In World War II, appeals to duty activated many to enlist voluntarily and those who didn't were quiet about it. During the Vietnam War, the threat of severe sanctions has not deterred open and organized opposition to the draft. In fact, some student groups have themselves attempted to activate commitments to "higher" values by urging the duty *not* to serve. The price authorities pay for losing political confidence is a loss in their ability to activate commitments and the necessity of relying on more costly types of social control.

The activation of commitments, then, depends on the existence of political trust but it becomes an even more powerful control when it is mediated by face-to-face interaction. This point is best demonstrated by a series of social psychological experiments going back to the early 1940's. These experiments, particularly the later ones in the series, have shocked and outraged many people and have stimulated a vigorous debate among social psychologists on the proper ethics in experimenting with human subjects. But whether or not such experiments *should* have been conducted, the fact is that they *have* been and their results are both surprising and instructive.

Jerome Frank (1944) designed a series of experiments aimed at exploring the conditions under which subjects would refuse to continue disagreeable or nonsensical tasks. Under some conditions, the experimenter simply told the subject what he was expected to do and this was sufficient to ensure performance. For example, some subjects were asked to perform the task of balancing a marble on a small steel ball; almost all of them continued to pursue this manifestly impossible task for a full hour with no overt resistance in spite of inward annoyance. Frank quotes one subject: "I was griped all the way through . . . [but] I promised a man I'd help him out and I couldn't see any reason for backing down on my word." In another variation, Frank attempted to get subjects to eat unsalted soda crackers. When they were told that the experiment required them to eat 12 crackers, the subjects all ate them without argument or protest.

However, in another condition, the situation was translated from one of social control to one of influence. Subjects were told, "This is an experiment in persuasion. I am going to try to make you eat 12 crackers in the first row on the tray. Whether you eat them or not is entirely up to you and doesn't affect the experiment one way or the other. But if you resist, I shall try to make you eat them anyway." Under such instructions, considerable resistance was produced and while verbal pressure from the experimenter succeeded in making several subjects eat a few more crackers, less than a third ate all 12 crackers. As an influence situation, the eating of crackers became a test of wills; as a social control situation, it simply involved the activation of the commitments involved in agreeing to be an experimental subject and no resistance was encountered.

At the point of refusal in the influence variation, the experimenter attempted to introduce legitimacy, by saying, "The experiment requires that you eat one more cracker and that will be enough," or "If you eat just one more cracker, that will be enough." These instructions were successful in getting two thirds of the recalcitrant subjects to take one more cracker. Eating the final cracker was seen as a way of terminating what had become an embarrassing and extremely awkward situation.[3]

Some other experiments show this form of social control even more dramatically. Pepitone and Wallace (1955) asked subjects to sort the contents of a waste basket which contained cigar butts, soiled paper, dirty rags, broken sticks,

---

[3]For a discussion of the particular role of embarrassment in such experiments and an ingenious experimental demonstration and theoretical discussion of how it operates in social influence situations, see Modigliani (1966).

pieces of glass, damp kleenex tissue, sodden purina chow, and other disgusting debris. The results were essentially the same in a variety of experimental conditions—the subjects snickered and laughed, and then got down to work and sorted the garbage with no strong protestations.

Martin Orne and his associates (1962; 1965) stumbled onto similar results in pursuing research on hypnosis. Orne sought a task which an unhypnotized subject would break off but not because of pain or exhaustion; that is, the task needed to be so boring and meaningless that a normal subject would simply refuse to do it after awhile. He found it extremely difficult to design such a task because of the powerful social control operating in face-to-face interaction with an experimenter who is accorded legitimacy. In one experiment, Orne gave the subjects a huge stack of 2,000 sheets of simple additions, each sheet containing 224 such additions. The simple instruction of "Continue to work; I will return eventually," was sufficient to get them to work for many hours with little decrement in performance. It was necessary for the weary experimenter to break off the task for the even wearier subject might have complied indefinitely. Even the addition of instructions to tear each sheet up into 32 pieces and to throw them away upon completion did not lead to significant resistance. When work stoppage occurred, the return of the experimenter to the room with instructions to continue was sufficient to ensure more work for additional hours.

Thwarted in this attempt to produce a breakdown of social control, Orne moved to more extreme tasks. Is the degree of control in hypnosis, Orne asked, actually any greater than the degree of control which an experimenter exercises over a normal waking subject when this subject accepts the legitimacy of the experimental situation? To test this, Orne and Evans (1965) used a series of tasks which were extremely disagreeable, and potentially harmful to either the subject himself or to others. The experiment called for a special apparatus—a box with a glass screen which could be slid into place and removed but which, because of the lighting and the type of glass, was impossible to see. Hypnotized subjects were compared with a group of unhypnotized subjects who were instructed to pretend they were hypnotized and with other control groups of normal waking subjects.

Initially, subjects were asked to pick up a few harmless objects from the box—with the glass screen not in place, of course. Then, a harmless lizard was placed in the box and subjects were told to pick it up, followed by similar instructions for a 14-inch harmless green snake and a 14-inch venomous black snake, capable of inflicting a mortal wound. However, before the last task and unknown to the subject, the invisible glass screen was silently lowered into place so that subjects who attempted to comply would get only bruised knuckles instead of snake bite.

At this point, the box was removed and the subject watched the experimenter pour concentrated nitric acid into a small shallow beaker. The experimenter dropped a coin into the acid and allowed the subject to watch it dissolve for approximately a minute. He then asked the subject to remove the coin with his bare hand and to plunge both coin and hand into a nearby basin of soapy, lukewarm water. If the subject complied (or if he did not comply, while he was diverted in some fashion), the beaker with acid was switched with one that appeared identical but contained a harmless solution. The experimenter then instructed the subject to throw the acid in the face of the lab assistant who had been helping with various aspects of the experiment. This completed the experiment proper and was followed by a fairly extensive postexperimental interview.

The results show a good deal of compliance with the experimenter's requests in all conditions. Of the six hypnotized subjects, five complied with all requests; the sixth, a young lady, became hysterical at the sight of the harmless lizard in the beginning and the other tasks were not used. All six of the subjects who were simulating hypnosis complied fully, carrying out all of the experimenter's requests although showing reluctance at a number of points. Of a group of six control subjects who were told that they were normal controls for a hypnosis experiment, five performed the acid tasks and three of the six attempted to pick up the venomous snake.

The latest and most significant work in this genre is that of Stanley Milgram (1963; 1964; 1965). Milgram focused his work on destructive obedience—obedience to demands which injure others. The basic experiment involves a naïve subject who administers what he believes are extremely severe electric shocks to another "subject" who is in fact a confederate of the experimenter. The subject believes that he is participating in an experiment which involves the effect of punishment on learning. He is instructed to raise the shock level administered after each error which the victim makes in a learning task involving the pairing of words. The simulated generator which the subject uses is extremely convincing; it is marked with voltage designations from 15 to 450 which are accompanied by verbal designations of slight shock, moderate shock, strong shock, very strong shock, intense shock, extreme intensity shock, Danger: severe shock, and two more positions ominously marked XXX. When the naïve subject pulls the generator switch, the generator lights and buzzes but, unknown to him, no shock is actually transmitted.

In Milgram's original experiment, the victim-confederate was in an adjacent room providing answers by pushing buttons. At the 300-volt level and again at the 315-volt level, he was instructed to pound on the wall and, thereafter, provide no more answers. Subjects typically turned to the experimenter at that point who advised them to treat no response as an incorrect response and to proceed with the shock schedule. If the subject asked about injury to the victim, the experimenter replied, "Although the shocks can be extremely painful, they cause no permanent tissue damage."

The results of this experiment are startling. Of the 40 subjects, all proceed past the strong and very strong shock readings and none break off before reaching 300 volts. Even more startling, 26 of the 40 reach the maximum level of 450 volts—

the XXX category. Such behavior is clearly not sadism. Subjects are under considerable stress and manifest it by sweating, stuttering, uncontrollable laughing fits, trembling, and other manifestations of extreme tension. Milgram quotes one observer:

I observed a mature and initially poised businessman enter the laboratory smiling and confident. Within 20 minutes, he was reduced to a twitching, stuttering wreck who was rapidly approaching a point of nervous collapse. He constantly pulled on his earlobe and twisted his hands. At one point, he pushed his fist into his forehead and muttered "Oh, God. Let's stop it." And yet he continued to respond to every word of the experimenter and obeyed to the end (Milgram, 1963, p. 377).

Why do subjects continue to honor a presumed obligation to an experimenter whom they do not know, to accomplish goals which are at best vague and obscure to them and which at the same time involve virtually gratuitous injury to another human being whom they have no reason to dislike? Variations of the experiment point to the fact that the strength of the obligation is heavily influenced by the physical presence of the experimenter. In one condition with 40 fresh subjects, the experimenter leaves after presenting the initial instructions and gives subsequent orders over the telephone. Where 26 of 40 were fully obedient when the experimenter was present, only 9 of the 40 subjects were fully obedient when the orders were conveyed over the phone. In a number of cases, the subject lied to the experimenter, saying that he was raising the shock level when he was in fact using the lowest level on the board. If the experimenter appeared in person after the subject refused over the telephone, he was sometimes able to reactivate compliance with the simple assertion, "The experiment requires that you continue."

Similarly, when the victim is brought into the same room with the subject, the number of obedient subjects goes down. The conflict becomes more intense for the subject with the experimenter looking at him and clearly expecting him to continue, while the victim very visibly indicates his pain and

his desire to participate no longer. Such results suggest that
the blindfolding of a condemned prisoner may have another
meaning than the one usually attributed to it. It is not so
much to protect the victim's feelings that a blindfold is
needed but rather to protect the executioner from his surveillance.

The basic mechanism of control accounting for these results is the activation of commitments. By conveying the
definition of the situation that the experimenter is a mere
agent, carrying out the sometimes unpleasant demands of
"research" or "science," he creates a situation where a refusal
is an act of deviance. Well-socialized subjects who have volun-
teered their services find it difficult to commit such an act
under the very eyes of the experimenter, but when they can
do it without the embarrassment of a direct confrontation, it
is much easier.

Perhaps the most powerful and common means of social
control is simply the conveying of expectations with clarity
and explicitness coupled with clear and direct accountability
for the performance of such expectations. As long as legitimacy is accorded in such situations, individuals will regard
their noncompliance as a failure and any interaction which
makes such a personal failure salient is embarrassing, unpleasant and something to be avoided.

This point is no less true for complex, modern societies
than for small communities. The activation of commitments
still depends both on the acceptance of a general obligation
and on reminders of what that duty is in specific situations.
The connections between the top political leaders in a society
and the members of a solidary group may be remote and may
pass through many links before they reach a person's boss or
neighbor or colleague or whoever else happens to do the re-
minding. Nevertheless, at the last link in this chain between
authorities and potential partisans, the desire to avoid the
embarrassment of being derelict under surveillance is a powerful persuader. The possibility of losing such a potent means
of control is a strong incentive for any set of authorities to

achieve or maintain high trust on the part of potential partisans.

PARTICIPATION AND COOPTATION

One of the most interesting and complicated of control mechanisms is cooptation. Essentially, it involves the manipulation of access, but as a control technique it is double-edged. In his classic study of the Tennessee Valley Authority (TVA), Selznick (1953) defined it as "the process of absorbing new elements into the leadership or policy-determining structure of an organization as a means of averting threats to its stability of existence." Earlier I argued that authorities normally will prefer to limit access to those elements most susceptible to control, but cooptation involves yielding access to the most difficult and threatening potential partisans. Why should any organization wish to deliberately create control problems for itself?

This mechanism arises in situations where control is already insufficient. It is a response to anticipated or actual pressure from partisans of such magnitude that it threatens the incumbent authorities and perhaps threatens the continuation of the system itself. Bringing such partisans "inside" does not create control problems; it simply transfers the existing ones to a different arena. In particular, while cooptation removes some of the insulation between potential partisans and authorities, it makes the former subject to other control techniques which were previously not available. Representatives of the partisan group, once inside, are subject to the rewards and punishments that the organization bestows. They acquire a stake in the organization, having gained some control over resources whose continuation and expansion is dependent on the organization's maintenance and growth. New rewards lie ahead if they show themselves to be amenable to some degree of control; deprivation of rewards which they now enjoy becomes a new possibility if they remain unruly.

Besides these changes in the situation of the partisans,

they are likely to enjoy some changes in orientation as well. First of all, their attitudes and commitment to the system may change. They may come to identify with the collectivity to such a degree that it will mute and subdue their original loyalty to a hostile outside partisan group which is trying to change the organization.

A desire to increase the potentialities for control lies behind the advocacy of admitting Communist China to the United Nations for many who hold such a position. UN membership is regarded less in terms of the access to influence it provides and more in terms of the control opportunities it offers. A hostile China is viewed as a greater threat outside the United Nations than inside. Once inside, it is argued, China would acquire interests which would make it a partner in maintaining the stability of the international system. It lacks such interests as an "outlaw" with relatively little stake in maintaining peaceful and cooperative relations with other countries.

From the perspective of potential partisans, cooptation must be regarded as a risk. Representatives of coopted groups are likely to be charged with having "sold out" at the least indication that they are pressing the group's demands with less vigor than previously. In fact, there is a tendency for such partisans to regard the entire opportunity for increased access as a form of manipulation. "The more a ruling class is able to assimilate the most prominent men of the dominated classes the more stable and dangerous is its rule," Marx argued. The very act of accepting access by a leader may be taken as evidence of desertion to the enemy either for selfish gain (i.e., as a "fink") or through naïveté (i.e., as a "dupe").

What can a potential partisan group hope to gain by allowing itself and its leaders to be coopted? It can gain increased access to resources which will enhance its influence and bring about outcome modifications. In other words, cooptation does not operate simply as a control device—it is also likely to involve yielding ground. For this reason, there are likely to be parallel fears on the part of authorities. They may worry that the act of cooptation represents the "nose of the camel" and be fearful of their ability to keep the rest of the camel out of the tent. Far from manipulation, some authorities may regard it as an act of undue yielding to pressure and the rewarding of "irresponsible" behavior.

Both the partisan's and the authority's fears about cooptation are valid fears. Cooptation invariably involves some mixture of outcome modification and social control and the exact mix is difficult to determine in advance. The authority who opposes coopting the hostile element fears that outcome modification will dominate the mix; the partisan who opposes accepting it, fears that the social control element will dominate.

The TVA case described by Selznick (1953) is instructive in this regard. The newly founded organization was faced, in 1933, with a powerfully entrenched existing interest bloc in the Tennessee Valley. This bloc consisted of a complex headed by the Land Grant Colleges, the more prosperous farmers represented by the American Farm Bureau Federation, and the Federal Agricultural Extension Service with its county agents. In some fashion, TVA had to confront this bloc whose territory the new organization was invading. Had TVA been firmly established with assured support of its own, it might have considered a strategy which would have challenged this bloc. In trying to become established, an alternative strategy recommended itself—to coopt the Farm Bureau complex into TVA. This policy was justified under the rubric of the "grass roots policy" which emphasized partnership with local groups in the region. The most significant act of cooptation was the appointment of one of the leaders of the Farm Bureau complex to TVA's three-man board.

One of the consequences of the cooptation strategy was a considerable amount of influence by the Farm Bureau complex over TVA's agricultural policies. Decisions on fertilizer programs, on the degree of emphasis on rural cooperatives, on the place of Negro farmers in the TVA program, were apparently all heavily influenced by this partisan group in the valley. On the other hand, TVA was able to carry out successfully its public power program and a number of other important objectives which might have become the target of active opposition if the Farm Bureau complex had not been coopted. It is never easy to assess whether the "price" in outcome modification was worth it or not, especially since one cannot know what would have happened if cooptation had not been used. The lesson to be drawn from the TVA example is not that it acted wisely or foolishly in coopting the Farm Bureau complex. Rather it is that *any* act of cooptation of potential partisans by authorities is likely to be a mixture of modification and social control and the balance of the mix is problematic and of concern to both parties.

Leeds's discussion (1964) of the absorption of nonconforming enclaves again illustrates the double-edged nature of this process. General Chennault and his followers in the period preceding World War II attempted to develop a group of trained fighter pilots (the "Flying Tigers") to furnish air support for Chinese land forces opposing the Japanese. The military had yet to accept, at this time, the full significance of air warfare and tended to regard it as auxiliary to infantry and artillery. Consequently, the allocation of supplies and personnel to Chennault were limited and a variety of other means were used to control and isolate the Flying Tiger group. However, after the U.S. entry into the war, this conflict proved too costly and a different control technique was used to deal with the rebellious group. In July, 1942, the American Volunteer Group of Flying Tigers was transformed into China Air Task Force and inducted into the U.S. Air Force under General Bissell. Later the group became the 14th Air Force under General Stillwell who was instructed to give Chennault full support. This ended the rebellion and removed the acute pressure from this partisan group. Along with the development of military technology and the experiences of the war, this absorption contributed to a major reorientation in the military toward the importance of air warfare. As in the

TVA case, cooptation seems to have involved large amounts of influence for the coopted group.

Closely related to the issue of cooptation and protest-absorption is that of participation in decision making. A long line of social psychological experiments in laboratory and field settings has emphasized the importance of participation as a positive factor in the acceptance of decision outcomes. It is not always clear precisely what is meant by participation.

One may emphasize the influence aspects of participation. To increase the participation of a group of potential partisans may mean to increase its influence over decisions. If there is increased satisfaction in such situations, it is because the modified outcomes are closer to what the partisan group desires. It may have very little or nothing to do with the fact of participation itself. If the significance of participation stems from the attendant influence, then we should expect the same increase in satisfaction and commitment that we would get if outcomes were similarly modified without an increase in participation.

Participation has a social control aspect as well. Here it is claimed that the act of participating in a decision process increases commitment and acceptance of decisions even if outcomes are no more satisfactory. The classic case of such alleged "participation" effects is the Hawthorne Study (Roethlisberger and Dickson, 1939) in which output increased following a variety of decisions made by a group of workers. These particular experiments are a weak reed on which to base any conclusion as Carey (1967) demonstrates in an appropriately harsh review. Carey argues that a "detailed comparison between the Hawthorne conclusions and the Hawthorne evidence shows these conclusions to be almost wholly unsupported" (p. 403). But in a later, more careful study of "participation" effects, Coch and French conclude that resistance to changing work methods can be overcome "by the use of group meetings in which management effectively communicates the need for change and stimulates group partici-

pation in planning the changes. Such participation results in
higher production, higher morale, and better labor-manage-
ment relations" (1965, p. 459).

Much of the small group work on "democratic" methods
of decision making has a strong social control emphasis. As
Verba points out,

Participation is in most cases limited to member endorsement of decisions made by the leader who . . . is neither selected by the group nor
responsible to the group for his actions. In group discussions, the leader
does not present alternatives to the group from which the members
choose. Rather, the group leader has a particular goal in mind and uses
the group discussion as a means of inducing acceptance of the goal. . . .
As used in much of the small group literature, participatory democratic
leadership refers not to a technique of decision but to a technique of
persuasion (Verba, 1961, p. 220).

Participation, like cooptation, is most likely to be some
mixture of influence and social control. Many of the same
issues arise. If the social control emphasis is paramount, partisans are likely to regard the process as pseudo participation
and manipulation. But it is not easy to increase participation
without also increasing influence. The increased access may
be intended to lead to a greater feeling of participation and
increased commitment of members, but those who are so ad-
mitted may not be very long satisfied with the trappings of
influence. When conflicts arise, the new participants may be
in an improved position to pursue their interests effectively.

By the use of *selective* participation, authorities may control some partisans by increasing the ability of others to influence. Hard-pressed authorities may welcome influence attempts by rival partisans for such influence may free rather
than confine them. Under such circumstances, authorities
may encourage increased participation by selected groups
despite, or even because of, the increased influence that it
will bring. The new pressures can then be pointed to as justification and defense for failure to take the actions desired by
the first group; the second group in turn can be brought to

appreciate the constraints which their rival places on the authorities.

The playing off of one partisan group against another as a technique of control is an ancient and familiar one. Machiavelli recommended it to his authorities and Simmel developed it in his discussion of the "tertius gaudens," i.e., the third party who draws advantage from the quarrel of two others. It is captured in the admonition to authorities to "divide and rule." Simmel illustrates it by describing the Inca custom of dividing a "newly conquered tribe in two approximately equal halves and [placing] a supervisor over each of them, but [giving] these two supervisors slightly different ranks. This was indeed the most suitable means for provoking rivalry between the two heads, which prevented any united action against the ruler on the part of the subjected territory" (Simmel, 1950, p. 165).

Such a control technique has certain dangers. First, while it may forestall the necessity of immediate outcome modification and increase the temporary maneuverability of authorities, it does not relieve the pressure in the long run and may even intensify it. For the moment, some of the resources of the partisan groups may be redirected into the conflict with each other but the authorities, by definition, control the choices which these groups are attempting to influence. Second, it is typically the case that rival partisan groups have some degree of common interest. If so, they may find it convenient to pool their resources in a temporary coalition. Thus, increased participation may lead to an enhancement of the influence it was intended to prevent.

Note that in the above discussion we are viewing organizational officials in their role as authorities. As partisans, these same individuals may desire increased influence for members of the same partisan group. The chairman of a state political party may argue for the widest possible citizen participation in the selection of delegates to the nominating convention because he believes that his own preferred candidate has a stronger following among the party rank and file than among the organizational regulars. In encouraging such rank and file participation, he is acting as a partisan attempting to influence the decision on selecting a candidate, not as an authority trying to minimize partisan influence on the decisions over which he personally exercises authority.

SUMMARY

This chapter has emphasized the perspective of authorities on the possible attempts of partisans to influence the outcome of the decisions they make. The central problem from their standpoint is the containment of influence. Pressure from potential partisans can be relieved by yielding ground and modifying the outcome of decisions or by dealing with the source of pressure through some form of social control.

One form of control involves the insulation of decision makers from potential partisans. This can be done at the point of entry by selecting those who will not present problems or at the point of exit by expelling recalcitrant individuals or groups. Once in, potential partisans are subject to a wide variety of sanctions. Finally, the orientation of potential partisans can be controlled by manipulating information, ideology, image of authorities, friendship ties, norms, and values. If potential partisans are sufficiently socialized and have high political trust they can be controlled by the activation of commitments. Mechanisms like cooptation and participation seem to involve a mixture of outcome modification and social control as a way of dealing with particularly powerful or threatening partisan groups.

There is a major difference in the influence and social control perspectives on the meaning and significance of social conflict. The social control perspective leads to an emphasis on stability. Conflict, under this view, represents a failure of social control—the failure to contain influence.

This is not to suggest that stability, as used here, is a bad thing. The authorities in whose maintenance one is concerned may be a progressive administration, vigorously pursuing land reform and providing effective leadership in a wide variety of ways. Or, they may represent a totalitarian regime relying heavily on terror and repression as social control techniques. In any case, the questions which arise from this perspective focus us on the manner in which authorities are left free to govern.

The influence perspective on the other hand leads to an emphasis on change. Conflict has a different meaning. Rather than a failure of social control, it is likely to be viewed as part of a social movement aimed at changing the content of decisions, the incumbent authorities, or the regime itself. Such potential partisans might be revolutionary or counterrevolutionary, progressive or reactionary. Again, no implication is intended about the desirability of change per se.

Perhaps the emphasis on stability in one perspective and change in the other is avoidable. Yet it seems to flow from the kinds of questions which arise naturally with each perspective. By taking both perspectives, one can avoid the characteristic blind spots of each one taken alone.

7

Predicting attempts at influence

When will potential partisan groups translate their potential
into action? What kinds of issues will mobilize them and,
once mobilized, what means of influence will they use? Answers to these questions have been hinted or implied earlier
but this chapter explores them more systematically. In suggesting hypotheses, one variable at a time is considered with
an implicit *ceteris paribus*. The "other things," in this case,
refer specifically to the other variables considered in this
chapter. For convenience in presentation, the hypotheses are
stated in terms of solidary group actions but they are intended to apply to any other potential partisan unit as well.

Level of concern

*The more a solidary group is affected by an issue, the
higher the probability of its attempting influence.* Such an
obvious hypothesis should need no extended defense, but a
few related observations are in order. A group's awareness of
how it is affected by an issue is subject to social control. By
the management of information and communication (inten-
tional or unintentional), authorities may partially determine
the definition of issues and this definition, in turn, may make
the awareness of important effects more or less likely. In
addition to the actions of authorities, the inherent complexity
of issues and the communication opportunities and skills
within a solidary group make the development of the awareness of effects problematic.

It is an important function of interest groups to articulate the effects of issues on solidary groups. Therefore, a subsidiary hypothesis states that: *The greater the interest group representation of a solidary group, the higher the probability of its attempting influence.* This latter hypothesis may be true in part because of the increase in capacity which interest groups provide through organization of resources. It is offered at this point because of the contributions that interest groups make to the *awareness* of being affected by the actions of authorities.

Since actors are differentially affected by decisions, we would expect different sets of active partisans on different issues. If we found a pattern in which active partisans had little overlap between issues, we could hardly draw conclusions from this fact about the diffuseness of the "power structure." In New Haven, for example, Dahl (1961) found one set of "influentials" on urban redevelopment, a second set on schools, and a third set on political nominations. It would be a mistake to conclude from this fact alone that New Haven has a "pluralistic" pattern of influence with different groups exercising influence in areas of limited scope. Given the proposition that people will attempt influence on those issues which affect them the most and the fact that issues affect people to different degrees, we should expect such differences in activity. As Bachrach and Baratz (1962, p. 950) point out in discussing the study of New Haven "it is evident from Dahl's own account that the Notables are, in fact, uninterested in two of the three 'key' decisions he has chosen." There is no need to invoke anything about *ability* to influence to explain the lack of overlap between decisions; differences in the *desire* or motivation to influence handle the job adequately. Additional evidence is necessary to establish a pluralistic pattern, for example, evidence on whether inequalities in the control of different kinds of resources are "cumulative" or "noncumulative" (cf. Dahl, 1961).

Amount and liquidity of resources

The greater the total amount of resources controlled by a

solidary group, the higher the probability of its attempting influence. This hypothesis suggests that the politically rich spend more than the politically poor. The more easily a group can afford to exercise influence, the more likely it is to do so. This idea is implicit in the concept of opportunity costs discussed in Chapter Four. The more resources that a group has, the fewer the alternative uses it most forego to exercise influence. A group with abundant resources is in a position to have its cake and eat it too.

The more liquid and uncommitted are the resources controlled by a solidary group, the higher the probability of its attempting influence. This hypothesis has a similar rationale. If resources are committed, their use on a new issue means some sacrifice. To mobilize and make them ready in a new arena may also involve some inconvenience and cost. Resources are more likely to be used if they require neither diversion nor conversion.

TYPES OF DECISIONS

Level of concern and amount and liquidity of resources are relatively straightforward and obvious variables affecting the probability of attempting influence. The bulk of this chapter will consider the variable of political trust and here the predictions and the argument become considerably more complicated. As a start, it is necessary to distinguish four different types of decision.

Decisions about scope of authority

Any set of authorities has some area in which they can make binding decisions. Some decisions affect the size of this area of authority. They might involve, for example, a public body taking on new functions previously performed by private individuals. The fluoridation of public water supplies involves the community taking responsibility for the prevention of caries, a dental condition which was previously handled, if at all, by private individuals in conjunction with their dentists. Caries is a pandemic but noncommunicable disease. Aside from any arguments about the safety or efficacy of water fluoridation as a preventive public health measure, people may disagree about whether it is appropriate for the community to take responsibility for the prevention of a noncommunicable disease. Such disagreement concerns the scope of authority that a community government should exercise.

It is possible, of course, for a fluoridation opponent to feel that it is perfectly proper and desirable for the community to add any and all nutrients or medication to the water supply as long as they are beneficial to health. Yet he might still oppose fluoridation because he doubts its beneficence. Apparently, most active antifluoridation partisans do not hold such a view. Rather, as Green (1961) suggests, they are likely to take a restricted view of the proper governmental role.

That fluoridation is an issue involving the proper scope of local government is illustrated by data from a study of community issues in 18 New England communities (W. Gamson, 1965; 1966a; 1966b). Interviews with active partisans on fluoridation and two other issues and with a sample of individuals reputed to be influential were culled for three kinds of statements: (1) Assertions that indicated a clear preference for a public as opposed to a private solution to a community need, or vice versa. (For example, "We should have a public garbage collection instead of having to pay a private company $12 a month.") (2) Comments that indicated that a particular objective can *only* or *never* be met through local government action. (For example, "Zoning laws are the only way we will ever be able to preserve the natural beauty of this town.") (3) Criticisms that the local government is invading areas of life which it has no right to regulate, that it is neglecting areas of life where it should regulate, or praise that it is acting as it should on these counts. (For example, "I don't think the town has any right to tell us what to do with our property," or "The Planning Board has got to do something about the uncontrolled growth on the West Side.")

If fluoridation is a scope issue, then we ought to find that proponents are more likely than opponents to make statements favorable to governmental solution and less likely to make statements which are unfavorable. Table 2 indicates that this is indeed the case. Among those proponents of fluoridation making codable statements, 77 percent are favorable to governmental solutions in general or on other issues besides fluoridation while only 20 percent of the opponents who make statements are sympathetic to such solutions.

TABLE 2

Preference for Governmental Versus Nongovernmental
Solutions by Fluoridation Position*

	Total Making Statements	Pro-fluoridation	Anti-fluoridation	Neutral on Fluoridation
Respondents making statements indicating a preference for governmental solutions	46 (46%)	24 (77%)	8 (20%)	14 (48%)
Respondents making statements indicating a preference for nongovernmental solutions	55 (54%)	7 (23%)	33 (80%)	15 (52%)
N =	101	31	41	29

*These are previously unreported data from a study described in W. Gamson (1965; 1966a; 1966b).

There are many other issues besides fluoridation which involve the scope of local government. Should a new school have a library and an extensive recreational facility or should it be kept to the bare minimum? Should the community attempt to implement a master plan that would regulate land use much more than it is presently doing? Should the community establish a housing commission to survey the needs for low-cost housing? All of these involve different conceptions of what the local government should be undertaking. Some individuals desire that the scope of local government should be minimal, providing nothing more than custodial services—a fire department, a police department, and a safe environment in which to go about their private pursuits. Others see the community government as an actual or potential outlet for the satisfaction of a variety of important needs. Consequently, many local issues are at least in part issues involving the scope of local government.

At the national level, a central theme in the protest symbolized by the Presidential candidacy of Barry Goldwater in 1964 was opposition to the increased scope of the federal government at the expense of state and local government and nongovernmental units. The New Deal brought a greatly expanded federal role and the scope issue was most central to opposition or support. For the most part, both major national parties have accepted the enlarged scope of the federal government but issues such as the federal provision of medical insurance for the aged, federal regulation of drugs and automobile safety, and federal aid to education, continue to involve differences on the proper scope of the federal government.

The small town insurance agent, real estate broker or physician who fears any increase in the area of federal control is not necessarily out of touch with reality or irrational. The federal government has become increasingly responsive to the needs of urban, industrial America and his distrust simply reflects his desire to see power reside in machinery which is more within his grasp. Fundamental to the distrust of federal power is the distrust of those groups who are seen as marshaling it—Negroes, Unions, immigrants. Why increase the power of a machine that one cannot drive?

While the Supreme Court is typically anathema to those who wish to limit the scope of the federal government, it may ironically turn out to have struck the greatest blow for "state's rights" through its reapportionment decisions. A major force behind the expansion of federal power is the inability of the metropolitan areas to handle their own problems—slums, unemployment, transportation, education. The federal rather than the state government is used in large part because state government is the citadel of small town control.

The reapportionment decisions have attacked this citadel. If it falls, we should expect an increase in the scope of state governments, because once this machinery is available to urban partisan groups, it is likely to be preferred for at least some former federally performed functions. It is a more inviting site since it is smaller and more accessible and, hence, more susceptible to influence. For example, where it is now the federal government that must help the cities with the modernization of their public transportation facilities, future solutions might well include a major role for state government. It will be a nice irony if the Supreme Court is the instrument of an increase in the scope of state governments at the expense of the federal government—a great victory for some of the Court's bitterest critics but, of course, a pyrrhic one.

Decisions about bias in procedures

Decisions about scope involve no change in the bias of political institutions or of the men operating them—they simply change the importance of whatever biases exist. This second category of decisions focuses on the bias inherent in political institutions. I will use the term "procedures" or "rules" as a shorthand expression to cover both structural arrangements and the formal and informal rules of operation used in producing decisions.

Fights over the rules of the game within which authorities operate can be among the most intense conflicts in politics. Rules are seldom neutral even though their effects may often seem obscure to the uninitiated. Outsiders may be puzzled about the intensity of a fight over whether local city elections should be held in a special election in the spring or at the same time as the regular election in November. But the minority party may view its chances as greatly enhanced by a special election which does not bring out the majority party faithful in as great proportions as the general election does. A shift from November to a spring city election is a shift in the bias of the election rules—or at least is perceived as such by the parties involved.

Nor is it surprising that some of the most historical power struggles in the House of Representatives have centered around the Speaker and the Rules Committee. The procedures by which a bill reaches the floor of Congress for a vote are fraught with implications for the influence of various partisan groups. Those which increase the authority of committee chairmen as gatekeepers on proposed legislation strengthen a bias toward potential partisans from one-party districts—in the South and in large, urban districts in the North, for example.

Many of the most critical fights in nominating conventions are on procedures. Should the adoption of the platform require a two-thirds vote or a simple majority? What should the order of the agenda be? What rules should the chair use to regulate debate? What should the order of voting be? All such questions, particularly if they are to survive the particular occasions, involve issues over who is favored to what degree by the rules. A rule which is regarded as "fair" is presumably one in which the major partisan groups accept the particular biases as balanced and, hence, as legitimate.

Finally, the issue of reapportionment is a classic case of a fundamental issue of bias in procedures. The slogan "one-man, one-vote" describes a situation no less biased than any other. It simply strengthens the bias toward majority rule. One must argue against it by invoking minority rights, an argument which is more difficult to justify when the particular minorities happen to be privileged ones, but nevertheless is based on a defensible principle. If one identifies with the solidary groups favored by reapportionment, then the degree of representation of rural and small-town voters is likely to be seen as "overrepresentation." But "overrepresentation" and "underrepresentation" are evaluations of biases which simply underline the fact that reapportionment is a *shift* in bias for various solidary groups regardless of how one evaluates the shift.

Decisions about personnel

Where issues of procedure concern bias in political institutions, this category concerns bias in the men who serve as authorities. Personnel issues involve the election or appointment of men to office. Questions about *how* men should be selected are procedural but given a set of rules, the actual selection of individuals is a personnel issue.

Every election is an issue of this type. Every primary or nominating convention, and every decision to appoint an official is as well. As with issues of procedure, *every* personnel decision involves some question of bias although it may *also* involve a question of competence. A disagreement about personnel or procedure might not focus on the handling of conflicts of interest. In many cases, the efficiency of the appointee or the procedure may be the critical concern, particularly in a highly integrated group where conflicts of interest are muted. Where conflicts of interest are more acute, every appointment must reflect some resolution of the bias problem—by appointing a man identified with a particular partisan group or a "neutral" figure. Neutrality may mean that his biases are unknown, undetermined, or balanced by his association with all major partisan groups or with none of them.

Decisions about content

This category is residual. It includes all of those issues that
do not concern changes in scope of authority or bias in procedures or personnel. This leaves quite a few issues, perhaps
the bulk of them for most decision-making bodies. Should a
new atomic reactor be located in Michigan or California?
Should a manned-bomber system be phased out? Should the
Smokemore Cigarette Company emphasize low tars and nico-
tine in their new advertising campaign? Should the land on
the north side of the new expressway be rezoned for industrial use? Should the city turn one of its parks into a parking
area? These are the staples of daily decision making. Some of
them may produce heated controversy while a great many
others are handled routinely by authorities in the absence of
influence attempts from potential partisans.

POLITICAL TRUST AND INFLUENCE

We take up the question of which partisan groups are most
likely to attempt influence separately for each type of issue.
For content issues and personnel issues, trust in authorities
will be critical; for procedure issues, trust in political institutions; and for scope issues, both kinds of political trust are
relevant.

Scope issues

*Solidary groups which are confident in the political institu-
tions and authorities and solidary groups which are alienated
from these objects will have a high probability of attempting
influence.* For the confident groups, influence will be exerted
to increase the scope of the authorities; for the alienated
groups it will be used to decrease the scope. The argument
for this hypothesis is obvious. It rests on the assumption that
groups will wish to see those authorities whom they trust
have as broad authority and as much control over their lives
as possible. Any body which can be depended upon to serve

as a faithful agent of one's interest ought to have its area of jurisdiction increased whenever possible. Efforts to reduce its scope should be resisted. Similarly, authorities which are working against one's interest ought to be put under as many restrictions as possible. Any effort to increase their area of control is threatening and should be the occasion for influence. Appropriations for the House Un-American Activities Committee are an example. We should expect influence attempts on the amount of the appropriation to come from the alienated and the confident groups in its environment.

There are three groups whose probability of attempting influence is low. *Solidary groups with neutral trust attitudes toward political institutions and authorities will have a low probability of attempting influence.* The scope of the authorities is not much of an issue for such groups. Neither an increase nor a decrease will make any difference since it creates no a priori advantage or disadvantage.

For different reasons, *ambivalent solidary groups will also have a low probability of attempting influence.* By ambivalent groups, I mean those who have one trust orientation toward political institutions and an opposing one toward the authorities. They might be confident in the procedures for making decisions but alienated from the incumbent authorities or alienated from the procedures in spite of confidence in the incumbent authorities.

Such ambivalent orientations are likely to be very unstable since the two attitudes are hardly independent. How much confidence in institutions can one have if they continue to allow hostile authorities to operate? Or, how unfair can such institutions be if they continue to allow one's friends and agents to operate in positions of authority? Nevertheless, such ambivalence may prevail during periods of transition in the political system and such a conflicting attitude is likely to keep such groups from making any effort on issues of scope. If they were inclined to act, the direction of their influence would not be clear. Should a confident alienated group work to increase the scope of the authorities in the hope that the trusted institutions will operate as a sufficient constraint on

hostile incumbents? Or should they work to decrease the
scope until such time as they can be assured of sympathetic
authorities? Should an alienated confident group work to
increase the scope of authorities in a context which limits the
ability of that body to produce favorable outcomes? The
difficulty of answering such questions will inhibit such groups
from attempting influence on scope issues.

*Other solidary groups will be intermediate in their proba-
bility of attempting influence on scope issues.* Groups which
are confident in the institutions and neutral toward the authorities or neutral toward the authorities and confident in
the institutions will favor increases in scope. Groups which
are alienated from the institutions and neutral toward the
authorities or neutral toward the institutions and alienated
from the authorities will favor decreases or limitation of
scope. These groups, in short, are like the pure confident or
alienated groups but are simply less clear-cut in their political
trust. Chart 2 summarizes the hypotheses on scope issues.

CHART 2

The Probability and Direction of Influence on Scope Issues as They
Vary with Political Trust

Trust in Political Institutions	Trust in Incumbent Authorities	Probability of Attempting Influence	Direction of Influence*
Confident	Confident	High	+
Alienated	Alienated	High	-
Confident	Neutral	Medium	+
Neutral	Confident	Medium	+
Alienated	Neutral	Medium	-
Neutral	Alienated	Medium	-
Confident	Alienated	Low	?
Alienated	Confident	Low	?
Neutral	Neutral	Low	?

  * A plus (+) indicates influence aimed at increasing scope, a minus (-) indicates
influence aimed at decreasing scope.

The above hypotheses are stated in terms of trust orientation toward a focal set of authorities. Frequently scope issues involve a question of whether one or another set of rival authorities should perform some function. An increase in scope for one group frequently is at the expense of some other group. The above hypotheses can be extended to such situations with very little effort. Instead of focusing on trust orientation toward a single group of authorities, the key variable becomes the *difference* in political trust. Those circumstances in which one is confident in both groups or neutral or alienated toward both groups are identical situations of no difference. A single hypothesis covers the situation here: *The greater the difference in political trust toward contending authorities, the greater the probability of attempting influence on issues over their relative scope.* As for direction of influence, solidary groups will support increases in scope for those authorities in whom they have the most political confidence. The probability of influence attempts would clearly be at its highest for a group which was alienated toward one set of authorities and confident in its rival. Note that this hypothesis about differential political trust focuses exclusively on trust in authorities and does not introduce trust in institutions as a variable.

Procedure issues

Before discussing the hypotheses here, it is important to distinguish two general classes of propositions. The first class relates general attitudes of political trust to probability of influence using only some very *general* information about the type of issue. It has the virtue of demanding very little knowledge about the content of the issue. But, of course, there is a price in accuracy for the minimum amount of information required in prediction. The second class of hypotheses utilizes more specific information about the particular issue involved. Depending on how specific this gets, the predictions are likely to be increasingly accurate but, at the

same time, they tend to become so obvious as to hardly war-
rant statement. In addition, the requirement of issue-specific
information is a demand which limits their applicability.

The following example illustrates these two classes of prediction. Imagine a group of French-Canadians in a Maine
community who feel that the city officials are dominated
by Yankees who disregard the needs of the French sector.
Knowledge of this general attitude is sufficient to make predictions about their attempts to influence the outcome of
city elections (a personnel issue). This is an hypothesis from
the first class and it will not enable us to explain the variance
in influence behavior by the French-Canadians in different
electoral campaigns. To do this, we must have additional
issue-specific information. This information might be that in
election A, a number of French candidates are competing
with Yankee incumbents. In election B, two factions of equally distrusted Yankees are competing. This additional information on issue-specific trust will allow us to avoid errors we
would make without it. In this case, our more general prediction of high activity by alienated partisan groups on personnel
issues would be even stronger for election A but would need
to be qualified for election B. The distinction between these
two classes of hypotheses should be kept in mind in the discussion which follows.

Trust orientation toward political institutions rather than
toward the men who apply them is critical for influence on
issues concerning changes in procedure. *Confident and alienated solidary groups will have the highest probability of attempting influence and neutral groups will have the lowest.*
For the confident groups, influence will be exerted to maintain the status quo; for the alienated groups, it will be used
to alter the existing procedures. An attempt to change the
rules is, for a confident group, a threat to the favorable bias
which it enjoys. Again it is worth noting that the bias is not
likely to be defended as such. Rather, an attempt will be
made to justify the existing rules on other grounds—that
they have worked well, that the time is not propitious for

correcting them because the organization is faced with an external crisis, that whatever the shortcomings of existing procedures, they have been mastered by everyone and changes would cause confusion, that they are hallowed by tradition, and so forth. Alienated groups are likely to initiate issues which involve extensive changes in the rules and to prosecute them vigorously, having no stake in the maintenance of existing ones. Neutral groups are likely to regard such arguments as technical or bureaucratic squabbles unworthy of their attention.

Any specific procedural proposal may produce exceptions to the above hypothesis. Clearly, we can expect groups to support favorable rules and oppose unfavorable ones and a normally neutral group might oppose a specific proposal which it viewed as creating an unfavorable bias. But the general predictions go beyond this obvious point and argue for the greater general salience of procedure issues for alienated and confident groups as opposed to neutral groups.

Personnel issues

Political trust toward the authorities rather than toward institutions is the critical variable here. *Confident and alienated solidary groups will have the highest probability of attempting influence and neutral groups will have the lowest.* Confident groups will tend to support incumbents and alienated groups will favor challengers. The justification, as for procedure issues, is more or less self-evident. For neutral groups, the bias of the authorities is not salient; for confident and alienated groups it is. The choosing of authorities is more likely to be an occasion for influence when bias is a concern as it is for the confident and alienated.

Again, it is possible to make more accurate predictions with issue-specific information. In choosing between rival sets of authorities, the relevant consideration for a potential partisan group is the difference in political trust felt toward the two groups. *The greater the difference in confidence which a solidary group feels toward two rival sets of candidates, the greater the probability of its attempting influence.* Note that this prediction requires information on attitudes toward two specific sets of authorities while the hypothesis in the paragraph above relies on generalized attitudes of trust toward a class of authorities.

Content issues

Up to this point, the hypotheses have suggested a higher probability of influence attempts for confident and alienated groups relative to neutral groups. For content issues, this prediction is reversed: *Neutral solidary groups will have a high probability of attempting influence and confident and alienated groups will have a low probability.* Content issues are those on which the general bias of authorities is taken as given. This bias determines for a solidary group the necessity and the difficulty of influence. A decision may affect one's most vital interests but if it is in the hands of trusted and reliable agents, then there is no need to spend resources to affect the outcome. A very good reason for remaining inactive is the confidence that one will be satisfied by the outcomes produced without doing anything.

In defining influence, two probabilities were contrasted. The probability before influence, P_b, gives us a precise way of conceptualizing the necessity of influence: $(1 - P_b)$. This necessity will be maximized when $P_b = 0$ and will be minimized when $P_b = 1$. Political trust is also defined by P_b where absolute confidence is represented by $P_b = 1.0$, neutrality by $P_b = 0.5$, and alienation by $P_b = 0$. It is clear, therefore, that alienation implies that the necessity of influence is at its maximum and confidence that it is at its minimum.

There is another good reason for remaining inactive on issues which do not affect underlying biases. If such biases are extreme enough, influence is useless or impossible. The less favorable the initial predisposition of authorities, the greater the amount of resources that will be necessary to move them to a particular probability or, in other words, the greater the cost of influence. The difficulty of influence is a reflection of how far P_b is from certainty, i.e., $1 - P_b$. The ease of influence is simply the complement of this or $1 - (1 - P_b) = P_b$. It follows that for confident groups, ease of influence will be maximized while for alienated groups it is minimized.

To complete the argument, the probability of a solidary group attempting influence on content issues may be viewed as a product of the ease and necessity of influence, but these variables are not independent. In fact, the probability of influence attempts, $P(I) = P_b(1 - P_b)$ where the first term represents the perceived ease of influence and the parenthetical term represents the perceived necessity. For confident groups, P_b approaches 1 and $P(I)$, therefore, approaches 0. For alienated groups, P_b approaches 0 and $P(I)$ therefore again approaches 0. $P(I)$ is maximized when $P_b = 0.5$ or, in other words, for groups that are neutral in their trust. To put the argument in words, for confident groups the probability of influence on content issues will be low because there is no necessity of influence; for alienated groups it will be low because there is no ease of influence; but, for neutral groups, the ease and necessity are in some balance and the result is to maximize the probability of influence attempts.

To put this hypothesis in perspective, we are arguing that confident and alienated groups will attempt influence on those issues where biases may be changed or the scope of authorities affected. They will not bother attempting influence on those issues where these matters are fixed. For neutral groups, the underlying biases are not an issue but on content issues which affect them, they can neither be sure of the outcome in the absence of influence nor need they fear that influence will be excessively costly or impossible. Chart 3 summarizes the predictions for procedure, personnel, and content issues and together with Chart 2 completes the hypotheses on political trust and probability of attempting influence on different types of issues.

CHART 3

The Probability and Direction of Influence on Procedure, Personnel,
and Content Issues as They Vary with Political Trust

Type of Issue	Trust in Political Institutions	Trust in Incumbent Authorities	Probability of Attempting Influence	Direction of Influence[1]
Procedures	Confident	- - - -	High	0
	Neutral	- - - -	Low	?
	Alienated	- - - -	High	*
Personnel	- - - -	Confident	High	0
	- - - -	Neutral	Low	?
	- - - -	Alienated	High	*
Content	- - - -	Confident	Low	?
	- - - -	Neutral	High	?
	- - - -	Alienated	Low	?

[1]A zero (0) indicates support for the status quo, i.e., existing procedures or incumbents. An asterisk (*) indicates support for change, i.e., new procedures or new authorities.

8

Means of influence, political trust, and social control

Political trust is not only related to the type of issue on which influence will be attempted but to the *means* of influence chosen as well. We have distinguished three means: constraint, inducement, and persuasion. All three are likely to be employed by a partisan group but any given group will tend to rely on one more than others.

IMPACT OF TRUST ON MEANS OF INFLUENCE

The propositions in this chapter have a strong parallel to those suggested by Etzioni (1961) in discussing compliance relations in organizations and we will draw heavily from Etzioni's arguments in justifying them. Etzioni distinguishes three types of social control by the officers of an organization over the organization's lower participants. The three types are only slightly different from the means of influence suggested here. Etzioni argues that the extent to which an organization will rely on one rather than another differs from organization to organization. Furthermore, "most organizations tend to emphasize only one means of [social control], relying less on the other two . . . The major reason for . . . specialization seems to be that when two kinds of [social control] are emphasized at the same time over the same subject group, they tend to neutralize each other" (Etzioni, 1961, p. 7).

163

The use of constraints, for example, affects the attitudes of authorities in such a way that persuasion is rendered more difficult. The resources required for persuasion are jeopardized or destroyed by threatening the authorities. The classic example of one means affecting another, Etzioni points out, is the difficulty of rehabilitation programs in prisons which emphasize the use of threats to maintain order and of therapy programs in mental hospitals where custodial problems are emphasized by the nonprofessional staff.

For similar reasons, the means of influence directed by a partisan group against a particular set of authorities will tend to emphasize a dominant means. What this means will be is determined by two factors: (1) whether the conditions currently exist for the most efficient and least costly use of this means of influence, and (2) whether the use of a particular means will affect the relationship with authorities in such a way that future costs of influence will be affected. Let us examine how this applies to the three states of political trust.

Confident groups

A confident solidary group will tend to rely on persuasion as a means of influence. For a confident group, the conditions for successful persuasion are maximized. The authorities, the group believes, are committed to the same goals and are viewed as its agents. On many issues, no influence at all should be required to bring about desired outcomes. However, because of the ambiguity of consequences of some decisions or because of a particularly strong personal concern, a solidary group may not be willing to accept even a favorable probability of a desired outcome without trying to improve on it further. They may fear, for example, that the blandishments of competing groups have obscured the nature of the particular issue leaving open the possibility of "error" on the part of well-intentioned authorities. But whatever the reason for influence, a confident group believes in the goodwill of authorities toward its interests and welfare. It is merely a question of implementing this goodwill in a particular case. This can be achieved through presenting information and arguments, drawing on the friendship and loyalty of the authorities, and activating their commitment to whatever collectivities and values the authorities and the solidary group share.[1] As Lane (1962, p. 144) describes the attitudes of his high-trust respondents toward influence, "The best way to use power is by persuasion; people shouldn't be forced to do things they don't want to do."

Persuasion may still have considerable costs even in such favorable circumstances. Political campaigns have long been recognized as occasions whose primary function is to activate the party faithful rather than to convert rival party members. To this extent, such campaigns may be viewed as an effort in persuasion by a partisan group (in this case the party leaders and activists), directed toward a set of authorities in whom they feel confidence (the party rank and file in the electorate). Such campaigns, of course, can be very costly in energy, money, and other resources despite their nature as efforts at persuasion. But whatever these costs of persuasion may be, they are likely to be less when aimed at a sympathetic group of authorities who are simply being asked to act in ways congruent with their own interests and values than when aimed at a group with different or conflicting interests.

Other means of influence, on the other hand, are likely to have adverse effects on the relationship between confident solidary groups and authorities. This is most obviously true in the case of constraints. To add disadvantages to the situation of the authorities or to threaten to do so may produce resistance. This resistance means that the general predisposition of authorities is changed so that it is less favorable to the interests of the solidary group on future decisions than it was in the past. In other words, constraints may result in a lowering of P_b for future decisions.

---

[1] I am speaking here of the group's perceptions of the authorities. In fact, such confidence may be misplaced and subject to change through subsequent experience with authorities.

It is possible to reduce this resistance by concealing the agency of the constraints, for example, by making the authorities feel someone else is responsible for the new disadvantages. Or resistance can be mitigated if the partisan is able to convince the authority that he has no personal discretion in his actions but is being compelled by outside forces or people and cannot, therefore, be held responsible. Schelling (1960) makes a similar point in emphasizing the use of commitment as a bargaining strategy. If one can convince the target that it is the *situation* which forces one's disagreeable actions, the resistance generated by constraints will be mitigated.

But even with mitigation, the repeated use of such a means of influence creates a poor atmosphere for efforts at persuasion. Constraints can undermine the persuasion resources which a group possesses. Such resources as reputation and personal attraction may be diminished or destroyed since they depend on the attitudes of the target of influence toward the group. Thus, some academic critics of American foreign policy with friends in the State Department are reluctant to engage in any public opposition to American policy. Efforts to discredit a policy and influence the public against it are a form of constraint. Those who feel that they have persuasion resources are reluctant to place them in jeopardy by actions which might alienate the officials whom they wish to influence. To the extent that such officials cultivate and encourage such beliefs without responding to influence, they are using a social control device which effectively contains influence attempts. Whether influence or social control dominates the mix is problematic and undoubtedly varies from case to case but it is useful to view the relationship from both sides. From the potential partisan perspective, confident groups will hesitate to use constraints on authorities because of the danger that such influence attempts will make future influence both more necessary and less easy.

The argument against using inducements is not as strong but is similar. While inducements are not as likely to cause

resistance, they may if they are offered too crudely and openly so that they are defined as a "bribe." But even when they
do not create resistance, they may lead to subtle changes in
the relationship which have undesirable consequences for the
future influence attempts of a group. This point is clearest
perhaps if we think of the partisan and the authority as close
friends. There is an important difference between the diffuse
reciprocal obligations of a friendship and the tacit bargains
and contracts of associates. An action carried out for the sake
of friendship does not imply any specific *quid pro quo;* it
is simply one of the demands that both parties to a relationship must accept to maintain it. But it is also part of the expectations of the relationship that neither party will exploit
the friendship by making such demands excessive. One is
sometimes reluctant to ask a friend for a favor precisely because he is not free to refuse as he would be in a more contractual, arm's length relationship. The diffuseness of the
obligation places a corresponding demand for self-restraint
on the parties if the relationship is to be maintained.

To offer a specific inducement to a friend is to violate the
norms of friendship. If one offers a *quid pro quo* for a favor,
it implies that one also expects a *quid pro quo* when he performs a similar favor. In general, it implies a different relationship in which each act of influence becomes a separate
transaction creating credits or debts for the parties involved.
If the partisan wants a favorable outcome he must not expect
to get it for nothing. If his credit is good, immediate payment
may not be required but at some time in the future he may
expect to be called upon to reciprocate. Such a shift in relationship involves a change in the initial predisposition of the
authority who must now be regarded as neutral in the absence
of influence instead of favorably predisposed as before. Thus,
as with constraints, by the use of inducements future influence will become both more necessary and less easy.

The situation is not basically changed if the basis of confidence in the authorities is not friendship but joint membership in the same collectivity. Again, to offer an inducement is

an implicit contradiction of the existence of this joint membership. If one is being asked to act in his own interest, which
he incidentally happens to share with the partisan making the
influence attempt, then why should he require an inducement
for acting? The offer suggests, instead, the separate and independent interests of buyer and seller. The seller has decision
outcomes which do not directly affect him and the buyer has
resources, the control of which the seller desires. In contrast,
a confident trust relationship suggests a set of commitments
which are not fully activated or a lack of information, but
the offer of an inducement implies the absence of such conditions. In doing so, it moves the relationship from confidence
toward neutrality and again increases both the necessity and
difficulty of influence.

Neutral groups

*A neutral solidary group will tend to rely on inducements
as a means of influence.* The proper conditions for persuasion do not clearly exist for such groups. The authorities do
not share the goals of the group but rather have their own set
of goals which do not necessarily conflict with or complement those of the solidary group. There is no a priori reason
for believing that the authorities will either favor or oppose
the outcome desired. There is no reason to feel that if the
authorities were fully informed about the consequences of
their prospective actions they would favor the alternative desired by the group. For them to recognize that a particular
choice will greatly satisfy such a group is no argument, in
itself, for making this choice.

If a group of authorities has control of something (a binding choice) that is unimportant to them and important to a
solidary group and the latter has something (inducement resources) that is important to authorities, then the conditions
for a successful transaction exist. While any given solidary
group may or may not have such resources, the first of these

conditions is implied in part by the neutral trust orientation. Such neutrality means that there is no reason to think that a decision which is important to the solidary group will be regarded as such by authorities; thus, it is available for appropriate inducements, felicitously offered.

With a neutral trust relationship, then, the proper conditions for inducements do exist but the proper conditions for persuasion do not. Constraints are again likely to have adverse effects for reasons identical to the ones given above. By creating hostility, they run the risk of changing the initial predispositions of authorities from neutral to unfavorable. The probability of favorable outcomes without influence may then become very low making future influence both very necessary and very difficult.

Alienated groups

An alienated solidary group will tend to rely on constraints as a means of influence. Such a group, unlike the others, has little to lose by constraints. Since the probability of favorable outcomes is already very low in the absence of influence, it is hardly necessary to worry about resentment. Such resentment does not materially increase either the necessity or the difficulty of influence. The attitude that "the only thing they understand is force" is a perfect manifestation of this trust orientation.

An appeal to an alienated group that it is "hurting its cause" by acts of constraint falls on deaf ears. Thus, to point out to poor Negroes in urban ghettoes that riots are resented is a rather irrelevant communication to a group which feels there is little likelihood of obtaining favorable actions from authorities in the absence of such riots. Civil rights leaders may deplore such actions because of their disapproval of violence per se and their concern about the direct injury to people and property which the riots produce. Furthermore, less-alienated groups within the Negro community may feel the loss of the ability to activate the commitments of authorities to shared norms against injustice and poverty. But the belief in such shared norms implies a confidence which the rioters presumably lack. For the extremely alienated, not only is there little to lose through generating resistance, but they can hardly be unaware that their major resources are constraints—the capacity to create trouble if their needs are not met.

The conditions for the successful use of other forms of influence are generally absent for alienated groups. It makes little sense to talk of persuading authorities who are viewed as systematically biased against one's interests. Such bias need not reflect hostility or even awareness of the solidary group's concerns; rather, it may simply stem from the fact that the authorities systematically favor a conflicting set of interests while maintaining a sense that they are acting fairly. But whether they are actively hostile or hold interests antagonistic to the alienated group, they are not likely to be persuaded by fuller information on the consequences of their choices. In fact, such information should persuade them to choose alternatives which are worse for the alienated group; confusion and lack of information is more desirable for it increases the chances of a favorable "error." Nor can the commitment of authorities to shared collectivities and values be appealed to because the alienated orientation assumes the lack of these.

The conditions for the use of inducements are not as obviously absent but are still lacking. Since the transactions referred to here are rarely if ever made the subject of explicit written agreements, they are built in large part on good faith. "You can't do business with Hitler," it used to be said, suggesting that even an exchange requires some degree of trust. This trust should not be confused with the more diffuse kind associated with friendship. It might be called, following Lieberman (1963), interest-trust or *i*-trust. This does not involve any belief in altruism or generosity on the part of the other party, only the belief that there is sufficient common interest for him to place the maintenance of a continuing exchange relationship over the specific advantage he might get by defaulting on any given transaction. But even such an *i*-trust is lacking for alienated groups who believe that the basis for such a neutral relationship is absent.

Some partial evidence

The hypotheses suggested above can be tested. I have tried to make them persuasive by argument and by illustration, but the examples do no more than establish a certain plausibility. There is one piece of more systematic evidence which, while it is far from definitive, does support the connection between the use of constraints and alienation. Almond and Verba (1965, p. 62) report the percentage of citizens in five countries who are alienated in their expectations about government outputs. These percentages run from 12 percent in the United States to 71 percent in Mexico with Great Britain, Germany, and Italy falling in between.

Rummel (1963) and Tanter (1965) have measured the level of internal violence in different countries. If we take this as a measure of the tendency of partisan groups to use constraints, then we ought to find that internal violence is positively correlated with the degree of alienation as measured by Almond and Verba. Tanter (1965) reports a factor analysis of nine measures of conflict behavior within nations: assassinations, general strikes, guerrilla war, major government crises, purges, riots, revolutions, demonstrations, and deaths by intergroup violence. He identified two factors which he labeled "turmoil" and "internal war." The turmoil factor offers a better measure of the frequency of constraints since it loads most highly on demonstrations, riots, assassinations, and general strikes.

Table 3 presents the factor scores for the five countries on which we have an alienation score. The two measures have a correlation coefficient of 0.69. Given the small number of countries involved and the very gross approximations of the variables of alienation and constraints, caution is clearly in order in interpreting this correlation. But at least it suggests that some more systematic support can be found for the hypotheses offered.

TABLE 3

Degree of Alienation and Frequency of Constraints for
Five Countries

Country	Percentage Alienated*	Constraint Scores**
United States	12	414
Great Britain	26	327
West Germany	26	60
Italy	42	604
Mexico.	71	701

$r = 0.69$

*These figures are from Almond and Verba (1965, Table II.10). They are contaminated somewhat for our purposes by the inclusion in them of "parochials" (individuals who are unaware of the impact of the government on their lives) in addition to "alienates" (individuals who have negative expectations about the impact of government).

**These figures are from Tanter (1965). They are the scores on "turmoil," a general factor with high loadings on demonstrations, riots, general strikes, and assassinations.

CHANGE IN THE TRUST ORIENTATION

In the discussion above, we have taken trust as the independent variable and have tried to use it to explain the choice of a means of influence. We now treat the trust orientation as itself subject to change and examine the impact of particular means of influence on such changes.

Successful influence

The hypothesized combinations of political trust and means of influence may be called *congruent* ones, i.e., alienation-constraints, neutrality-inducements, and confidence-persuasion. *Use of a congruent means of influence increases the strength and stability of the existing trust orientation if it is perceived as successful.* The connection between trust and choice of means is confirmed for a solidary group by successful use of congruent means. A confident group has its confidence reinforced by being able to persuade authorities. A neutral group has its neutral contractual orientation reinforced by concluding a successful transaction in which authorities have accepted some inducement. An alienated group is reinforced in its belief that only force is understood by the successful use of constraints. Note that this hypothesis contradicts a possible alternative one that successful influence increases confidence. Instead, it will be argued that successful influence may sometimes reinforce alienation rather than lessen it and that the effect of successful influence on political trust depends on the *means* of influence used.

Suppose that a noncongruent means of influence is chosen. It is such situations that produce shifts in political trust and these shifts can be in either direction. Chart 4 helps to make the direction clear.

CHART 4

Effect of Successful Use of Given Means of Influence on Political Trust

Trust Orientation	*Means of Influence*		
	Persuasion	*Inducements*	*Constraints*
Confidence	R	–	–
Neutrality	+	R	–
Alienation	+	+	R

Key: R = reinforces existing trust orientation.
     + = changes it in direction of increased confidence.
     – = changes it in direction of decreased confidence.

The use of a means of influence below the diagonal will increase confidence while the use of a means of influence above the diagonal will decrease it.

Use of a means below the diagonal involves the selection of a means which implies greater confidence than exists. If such influence is successful in spite of expectations to the contrary, it suggests that the original trust orientation was insufficiently confident. First take the case of a neutral group which successfully uses persuasion. It suggests that the common interest with authorities may be greater than had been allowed. They required no *quid pro quo* to take the desired action but were willing to do it without any special inducement or personal gain. They must, therefore, have had a predisposition to act in that direction which the influence attempt activated. But if the predisposition toward favorable action existed in this case, perhaps it exists more generally and one can expect favorable outcomes even without influence. Thus, the thrust of such an event is toward greater confidence.

An alienated group which successfully uses persuasion should be in for an even more abrupt shock. That the target of influence was willing to act favorably without being constrained to do so is difficult to explain. Perhaps the conflict of interests is not as total as had been believed and there is some coincidence of interests as well. Again a favorable predisposition is implied which contradicts the general belief that the initial predisposition is unfavorable. Of course, any particular instance can be simply treated as an exception but if such exceptions occur with any frequency or if they occur on issues regarded as critical, then they should create a push toward greater confidence.

Even an alienated group that used successful inducements should be pushed in this direction. If authorities whom one cannot do business with turn out ready to do business, then the initial belief is weakened. It is not that they are against us, a group might reason as a result, but only that they are for themselves. They are not malicious but only indifferent.

They are not our friends but at least they may be our venders. Again there is a shift away from alienation.

The successful use of a means of influence above the diagonal implies greater alienation than initially existed; it suggests that the original trust orientation was overly confident. All of these cases are interesting examples of situations in which successful influence may increase alienation. If a confident group must offer an inducement to gain a favorable outcome, something is amiss. The authorities should require no inducement to do what is in the mutual interest of partisan and authority. That they ask or accept such an inducement implies that such mutuality of interest is lacking. Can a favorable predisposition be said to exist if one must offer an inducement to activate it? At the very least, it must be a weak one and the greater the inducement necessary to produce a favorable outcome, the weaker the initial predisposition must be.

If a confident group uses constraints to gain a favorable outcome, the implication of overconfidence is even stronger. Presumably the authorities would act against one's interest if they were unconstrained but a confident trust orientation implies the opposite. Why constrain somebody to do something that he wants to do anyway? Presumably, because the authorities did *not* seem to want to do it and if unconstrained would have acted against one's interest. But this suggests that the initial confidence was unrealistic and pushes toward decreased confidence in the future.

A neutral group which makes successful use of constraints is also acting in a way contradicted by their trust orientation although the overall argument is least clear at this point. In a neutral relationship, influence involves reciprocity. Inducements are given and favorable decisions are received. But such reciprocity is absent in constraints. The authorities still give favorable outcomes but they receive nothing in exchange. For partisans to act in such a fashion is unfair dealing on their part unless they are dealing with hostile or biased authorities who deserve no better treatment. In other words, for a group to make such absence of reciprocity justifiable to themselves,

they must feel that a *quid pro quo* was not warranted and
deserved. This makes sense if the authorities are regarded as
themselves unfair and negatively biased. Thus, the successful
use of constraints by a neutral group pushes it toward an
alienated orientation.

Unsuccessful influence

It is not clear, given our arguments for the congruence of
certain combinations of means of influence and trust, why
noncongruent cases should ever occur. They do, of course,
and this requires some explanation. First of all, we do not
expect any group to make exclusive use of a single means of
influence. We have argued only that one element in the mix
will tend to be dominant and the particular element and its
strength will be determined by trust orientation. A confident
group should have a high probability of using persuasion, a
lesser probability of using inducements, and a still smaller
probability of using constraints.

Implicit in the occurrence of a successful noncongruent
influence attempt is the occurrence of a previously unsuccessful congruent attempt. The unsuccessful attempt may be
viewed as weakening the stability of the trust orientation
without changing its direction. It then becomes a question of
whether one moves to the right or left as one leaves the diagonal in Chart 4. Clearly this is only a question for neutral
groups; confident groups can only move above the diagonal
to inducements or constraints that will lessen confidence and
alienated groups can only move below the diagonal to inducements or persuasion that will increase confidence.

Which direction will neutral groups move in following an
unsuccessful use of inducements? The answer seems to rest
on the nature of the failure. We can imagine two situations:
(1) the authorities reject the inducements because they suggest that bargaining is improper, or (2) they reject the inducements because they suggest that they are insufficient. In the
first case, unsuccessful inducements should be followed by

persuasion attempts while in the second case they are followed by attempts at constraint. If the required inducements are exorbitant, it hardly suggests that an effort at persuasion will be successful. On the contrary, it implies the unlikelihood of favorable action if no advantage is added to the situation of the authorities. There is no such implication for the rejection of the bargaining process. While it does not imply that persuasion will be successful, it does suggest that the choice will be based on the orientation of the authorities and that it is appropriate to aim one's influence here rather than at their situation.

CHART 5

Effects of Unsuccessful Use of Given Means of Influence
on Political Trust

Trust Orientation	Means of Influence		
	Persuasion	Inducements	Constraints
Confidence	W	R	R
Neutrality	R	W	R
Alienation	R	R	W

Key: R = reinforced existing trust orientation.
      W = weakened existing trust orientation.

We have dealt with both successful and unsuccessful congruent attempts and with successful noncongruent attempts. This leaves us with unsuccessful noncongruent attempts. We may assume as before that instances off the diagonal imply unsuccessful previous congruent attempts. Unsuccessful noncongruent attempts, as Chart 5 indicates, have the predicted effect of reinforcing the existing trust orientation. The general argument for this set of hypotheses is that trust orientation creates an expectation that such means of influence are inappropriate and an unsuccessful use of this means confirms this expectation. This argument, however, is more convincing for the cases below the diagonal than for those above.

Below the diagonal of Chart 5 we have groups using a means of influence which implies a greater trust than they enjoy. It is not surprising to an alienated group that they are unable to .persuade or induce the authorities. This is what they have been led to expect and they simply find their original attitude confirmed. Similarly, a neutral group does not expect to get something for nothing; it should do nothing more than confirm this belief when they find they are unable to persuade. If we assume that a noncongruent attempt has been preceded by an unsuccessful congruent one, then the two unsuccessful experiences are offsetting. Trust orientation is weakened by the first but reinforced by the second and will remain unaltered by the influence experience.

It might be argued that unsuccessful influence attempts will decrease confidence but I am explicitly not arguing that here. Trust orientation is affected by the nature of the decisions made and the satisfaction or dissatisfaction with them. To the extent that unsuccessful influence attempts imply unfavorable outcomes, we would expect them to be associated with a decrease in confidence but this decrease comes from the bad outcomes rather than the experience of unsuccessful influence. The effect would be no different if influence had not been attempted at all and the same outcomes had resulted. However, political trust is affected not only by decision outcomes but also by influence experience and it is these hypothesized effects that are summarized in Charts 4 and 5.

SOCIAL CONTROL AND TRUST

The trust orientation of solidary groups is not only related to the means of influence chosen but to the social control response as well. Trust is relevant to authorities for two reasons: (1) It affects the means of influence a partisan group is likely to use. While all influence puts limitations on the freedom of authorities, constraints are particularly unpleasant because they add or threaten to add new disadvantages. (2) It affects the capacity of authorities to achieve collective goals. To the extent that they must make commitments without the prior consent of those who will ultimately be called on to supply the resources, they require high general trust.

Both of these reasons argue for the advantage to authorities of high confidence on the part of potential partisans. Furthermore, some systems require such confidence even more than others. Etzioni argues

Organizations that serve culture goals have to rely on normative [control, i.e., persuasion] because the realization of their goals requires positive and intense commitments of lower participants to the organization . . . and such commitments cannot be effectively attained by other [types of control]. . . . The attainment of culture goals such as the creation, application, or transmission of values requires the development of identification with the organizational representatives (Etzioni, 1961, p. 82).

When an organization must bring about some change in the orientation of the members, persuasion is the most appropriate technique. A heavy reliance on sanctions leads to a "calculative" involvement of members. "Manipulation of pay, fines, and bonuses does not lead to internalization of values," Etzioni writes (1961, p. 84). Insulation in such situations may lead to the containment of influence but interferes with or makes impossible high confidence.

Colleges and universities are recognizing increasingly that their means of control of students interacts heavily with the achievement of their educational objectives. One may contrast, for example, a small liberal arts college such as Antioch with a large, state university in their respective mechanisms of control. A university is a more complex organization and its control structure reflects the greater diversity of its goals. Heavy reliance on grades (i.e., sanctions) and the exclusion of students from major influence on educational policies (i.e., insulation) may effectively contain influence over large areas of decision but they do not seem as effective in producing high confidence in the university administration on the part of students. In contrast, Antioch college has included high participation by students in the affairs of the college for many years and justified it explicitly as part of its educational program. The higher trust generated by such participation may make *persuasive* controls more potent but it is probably less effective overall in containing the influence of students. However, the loss in controlling influence is compensated by the gain in trust; this trust, in turn, increases the ability of the college to give the students major responsibility for their own education.

The above example illustrates a central point: the "power" of a system to achieve collective goals is affected by the means of control employed. With an appropriate means of control, the system not only contains influence but increases its total resources; with an inappropriate means of control, it may contain influence but so consume its resources in doing so that it diminishes its effectiveness in achieving collective goals.

The desire to increase confidence, then, is one determinant of the type of control sought and this will vary with the requirements of the system for high member commitment. The existing trust orientation toward authorities is a second determinant because it affects the means of influence a group will use. These two factors are considered together as we examine the social control relationship toward groups with different trust orientations.

Confident groups

Authorities will tend to rely on persuasion as a means of control over confident solidary groups. The arguments here are a variant of the earlier discussion on means of influence. Persuasion is the means of control most consonant with build-

ing and maintaining a positive trust orientation. When initial
trust is high, a basis for persuasion exists. Confidence implies
that the solidary group is already persuaded of its common
interest with authorities. Persuasion only requires convincing
the group that the authorities have things well in hand and
that it will be well served without pestering the authorities
unduly on specific decisions.

Other means of control tend to reduce the confidence of
solidary groups. Insulation removes opportunities for the development and maintenance of confidence. Constraints as a
means of control create resentment toward authorities, reduce trust, and encourage the use of constraints by solidary
groups as a means of influence. Inducements, as argued above,
encourage a calculative and neutral trust orientation toward
authorities. In short, all means of control other than persuasion hinder the maintenance and development of high confidence, a doubly undesirable consequence. The resultant loss
of credit leaves the authorities less able to achieve collective
goals while at the same time it increases the probability that
constraints will be used against them as a means of influence.

Neutral groups

*Authorities will tend to rely on sanctions and particularly
on inducements as a means of control over neutral solidary
groups.* While persuasion still is valuable to the extent that
it can be used successfully, it is more difficult to use with a
neutral group. Authorities are cast more in the role of broker
or referee among competing groups. Inducements have a distinct advantage over constraints because they are less likely
to alienate the solidary group and, hence, less likely to produce constraints as a means of influence. As Pareto argued in
accounting for the shifts in control from "lions" to "foxes,"
force is used to better advantage *against* authorities in the
process of attaining power than against one's subjects in the
process of maintaining discipline when in power. Insulation

provides fewer protections against the development of alienation by a solidary group than does participation of the group
in a system of exchange.

Alienated groups

*Authorities will tend to rely on insulation as a means of
control over alienated solidary groups.* Insulation offers protection against the use of constraints by alienated groups. By
preventing their access to resources and their ability to apply
them, authorities can control the capacity of groups to use
constraints without altering their inclination to use them.

Other means of control offer difficulties of one sort or
another. Sanctions involve some access. Constraints used
against alienated groups have fewer disadvantages than when
used against neutral or confident groups because there is less
trust to be destroyed. Still, it is necessary for a group to have
something to lose before it can be subjected to effective constraints. Giving it something to lose can hardly be done without at the same time giving it some access.

Inducements are likely to be very costly with alienated
groups. Such groups do not operate in a spirit of compromise;
half a loaf does not appear better than none. As a consequence, authorities will find such groups unreasonable to bargain with and insatiable with respect to inducements. "Give
them an inch and they take a mile," is the classic expression
of such attitudes toward alienated solidary groups. Finally,
persuasion is difficult since it will tend to be regarded as lying
and manipulation. In short, insulation offers authorities the
most satisfactory protection from alienated solidary groups.

Social control and changes in trust

The above hypotheses relating trust to means of social
control suggest congruent combinations. Use of a congruent
means of social control, like use of a congruent means of

influence, maintains the existing trust orientation. The use of a noncongruent means tends to produce changes in trust.

A confident group can be moved toward neutrality or alienation by heavy reliance on sanctions and insulation. A neutral group can be made more confident by involving its members in relationships that increase identification with authorities and encourage potential partisans to internalize the authorities' goals. A neutral group can be made more alienated by heavy reliance on constraints and by insulating it from relationships that increase identification and internalization. An alienated group can be made more confident by involving it in a system of exchange with authorities and a series of relationships which encourage identification and internalization.

However, social control is only one of two responses available to authorities. They may also alter the policies they pursue. To the extent that the alienation of a solidary group is based on a realistic appraisal of the decisions produced by authorities, altering outcomes is a much more direct means of raising confidence. To remove insulation from an alienated group will surely make the control problems of authorities more acute if such groups continue to be systematically neglected in the decisions of such authorities. The best long-run strategy for authorities in building confidence concentrates on equity in allocating resources and effectiveness in generating them and makes social control a secondary consideration and by-product.

9

Some implications for social change

If the concept of influence is to remain useful, it should not be asked to do too much. Many things happen without influence being the cause. Influence, as used here, is not equivalent to anything that affects decisions but is reserved for the intended effects of actors upon the decisions of other actors. This leaves a great deal of explaining for such things as the demands of the physical environment, values, norms, social institutions, internal predispositions and the like. If we say that a voter is "influenced" in his voting choice by the beliefs of his deceased parents or by his religion and social class, we are not using the term influence in the narrower sense of this book. Rather, we are talking about certain social forces which operate upon his choice and create a context in which influence may or may not occur. These forces may be so great that there is little another actor can do to influence his vote and influence adds nothing to an explanation of why he votes as he does.

Bachrach and Baratz point out that influence is also "exercised when A devotes his energies to creating or reinforcing social and political values and institutional practices that limit the scope of the political process to public consideration of only those issues which are comparatively innocuous to A" (1962, p. 948). Cartwright (1965, pp. 19-20) covers such influence under the more general concept of "ecological control." "When O influences P by ecological control, he

185

takes some action which modifies P's social or physical environment on the assumption that the new environment will subsequently bring about the desired change in P." Such ecological control is covered by the concept of influence when the actions of partisan groups alter the probability of preferred outcomes. But the environmental forces which affect the decisions are not included. Only actors influence.

One can both overemphasize and underemphasize influence as a determinant of the actions of authorities. The overemphasis treats all decisions as if they were completely "free" and unconstrained by role requirements or by other limits on the freedom of authorities. This is a very easy trap for partisans to fall into. The limits may not be very visible to outsiders and the efforts of authorities to make partisans aware of such limits are often treated as rationalizations. A typical case is the authority who will not pursue a course of action because he says it "will not work." The partisan does not see this as reason for not trying it and, indeed, it is difficult for the authority to make a convincing case without demonstrating the limits of his freedom by violating them. He is reluctant to do this because it is costly and wasteful to him. It is this type of interaction that leads authorities to regard criticism from those without authority as "irresponsible." They mean that, not having to face the costs and personal consequences of proposed actions, the critics are able to treat choices as free and unconstrained by the social environment.

When influence is overemphasized as a cause of behavior, the failure to get a preferred outcome appears to be due to some rival who has exerted greater influence. If no such rival is visible, then it must be postulated as a hidden influence. An overemphasis on influence can easily lead to conspiratorial theories of events. By taking as a *premise* the fact that some group of actors are influencing the choices of authorities, one is necessarily left with covert influence as an explanation whenever noninfluence factors are really determining the actions.

The conspiratorial fallacy is the result of an overemphasis on influence but the underemphasis has an analogous fallacy.[1] This view plays down or ignores the impact of the decisions of authorities. Their choices are viewed as pseudo choices at worst and as trivial choices at best. Authorities have the illusion of exercising some personal discretion in decision, the argument runs, when in fact any person in their position would be led into the same choice. It is not uncommon for authorities to take this view of themselves. "If Barry Goldwater were President," a high-ranking Defense Department official once remarked during the Kennedy administration, "by the end of a few weeks he would find himself acting exactly as President Kennedy is acting." A Presidential candidate can hardly offer a choice when the hard realities of the situation make all incumbents echoes of each other.

Those who emphasize the technical nature of decisions sometimes adopt this illusory choice fallacy. By emphasizing the collective aspects of decisions and their complexity, any problem may be treated as involving a technical matter of the effectiveness of different alternatives in producing public goods. If a decision to plan a deliberate budget deficit is really only a matter of a sophisticated understanding of the economics involved, then opposition and charges of "fiscal irresponsibility" are simply matters of misunderstanding or superstition. Thus, many acts of influence on authorities are regarded as misguided and based on a lack of proper communication; the partisans fail to appreciate, in this view, the very limited maneuverability left after the range of choice has been greatly narrowed by the environment.

Underemphasis on influence is undoubtedly the more likely occupational hazard for sociologists. After all, a great deal of behavior can be explained by the social environment without invoking the intended influence of actors. If one were

---

[1]Cf. Mills's (1956, pp. 15-18) discussion of the "omnipotent" and the "impotent" elite.

interested, for example, in the relative amount spent on education by a series of communities, it might be possible to explain all or almost all of the variance between communities without invoking political decisions. Differences in resources available to communities may leave those who wish to upgrade the quality of their schools with little real opportunity to do so. It might be argued that a reasonable strategy of explanation is to first see how much one can explain without invoking decisions. Only when the impact of structural limits has been thoroughly explored should one analyze the process of influence upon decisions of other actors in the system.

Nevertheless, it is easily possible to underrate the significance of decisions. First, they may singly or in aggregate have far-reaching effects on the social structure and thus may change the kinds of limits that will operate on future decisions. And even small differences in choice can have very large consequences. No one could deny, for example, that the President of the United States has some choice about whom he appoints as an ambassador. At the point of making this choice, the President may be less concerned with competence than with the repayment of a political debt. Yet this ambassador's actions and advice may be critical in later decisions—as, for example, Ambassador W. Tapley Bennett's advice was in President Johnson's decision to send American Marines into a civil struggle in the Dominican Republic. Small differences in trajectory may produce very large differences when projected over time. Thus, there is danger in treating the choices of actors as irrelevant.

INFLUENCE AND SOCIAL CHANGE

Social change can come through a process of influence, but it can also come as a developmental outgrowth of societal processes. In the normal functioning of any complex social system, certain strains and tensions are generated. In addition, there is a problem of adaptation to an environment which is rarely fixed. Changes from these sources do not necessarily involve influence although most specific changes probably are the result of a combination of conscious decision and developmental forces.

Take, for example, the issue of the concentration of power in the hands of a small number of people. If we assume, for the sake of argument, that such a change has occurred in American society, there are explanations that invoke influence and those that do not. Without invoking influence, one can argue as Parsons (1960) does, that the demands of governing a mature, industrialized society and of meeting a changed U.S. role in the world create this concentration. The flow of personnel between the top echelons of the military, industry, and government may simply be taken as evidence of the interchangeability of the technical and managerial skills involved in different sectors. Power is concentrated, in this argument, not because any individual or group sets out to get it but because it is necessary for effective government, i.e., it works better. "Structural differentiation" is a prime example of a developmental change which does not stem primarily from the influence of partisans on authorities.

Social change may also occur through conscious, explicit decisions which alter the social structure. Laws are an example of such decisions. One might well argue that the major thrust of social change in the United States has been to subject more and more forces to the manipulation of conscious decision. Many forces which were taken as "given," as the uncontrollable set of limiting conditions for decisions, are now regarded as in part manipulable. This is nowhere clearer than in the economic realm where such things as fluctuations in the business cycle, growth rate, price stability, unemployment, and many other economic factors used to be regarded as the inexorable facts of life within which a government must work. Now, these forces have become the subject of conscious economic policy. The control is not complete, of course, but these forces are regulated and harnessed for certain ends.

An area of decision for one body or at one point in time

may become an environmental constraint for another body or for the same body at a different time. Yesterday's decisions represent commitments which serve as limits on today's decisions. Decisions at the national level may set conditions for lower levels. Thus, a state governor may simply have to accept a given rate of unemployment in his state as an inexorable fact even as the federal government attempts to deal with it through conscious economic policy. The essential point here is that change may occur through influence on a series of decisions which alter the social structure even though freedom of action is limited on *each one* by conditions which are, momentarily, taken as given.

Influence which leads to a rapid and major reorganization of society is most likely to come from an alienated group or collection of groups which constitute a social movement. The success of such a movement in bringing about social change must be regarded, from the standpoint of the authorities, as a failure of social control. If successful social control had been operating, then influence would have been contained and, at the least, change would have occurred more slowly. "Effective conflict regulation," Dahrendorf suggests (1959, p. 234), "serves to reduce the suddenness of change. Well-regulated conflict is likely to lead to very gradual change. . . ."

Major changes through the influence of social movements can occur for two reasons: bad decisions or social control errors. Authorities may make decisions which adversely affect such a large and influential group that even the most skillful efforts at social control are insufficient to contain influence. Or, the techniques of social control used may be so clumsy and ineffective that they stimulate rather than contain influence.

Partisan groups may try to increase their resources by deliberately trying to create an "error" in social control (that is, the use of an inappropriate control device which increases potential influence). Such errors may be quite important in accelerating the pace of change: it may lead a social movement to new allies and stronger commitment of its supporters, it may lead to the withdrawal of legitimacy and trust from existing authorities and thus weaken their ability to enforce decisions and make new commitments, and it may create such serious instability that many who were not convinced of the need for change will now find the status quo intolerable. In this situation, the natural advantage which accrues to those supporting the status quo switches to those who support change. A sense of this reversal has on occasion led revolutionaries to welcome a worsening of social conditions. They reason that the resultant crisis will weaken existing arrangements and thereby enhance the possibilities of social change. Unfortunately, many different kinds of changes may follow and the relative probability of changes that are deplored may be enhanced even more than the probability of desired changes.

While social control errors may accelerate the pace of change, a group which deliberately tries to create them is playing with fire. Political professionals, as Dahl (1961, p. 320) points out, "have access to extensive political resources which they employ at a high rate with superior efficiency. Consequently, a challenge to the existing norms is bound to be costly to the challenger, for legitimist professionals can quickly shift their skills and resources into the urgent task of doing in the dissenter."

Still, the application of social control is a delicate business, requiring great self-control and intelligence on the part of authorities if it is to dampen influence more than stimulate it. The shattered remains of many administrations and regimes testify to the fact that errors are made. It is worth examining some of these more specifically. Removal of partisan leaders by exile, imprisonment, or execution can backfire. It offers a movement with strong secondary leadership an opportunity to mobilize its supporters to the fullest and to draw in sympathetic bystanders, particularly if the pretext for repression is a weak one. But repression may be successful if the solidary group is sufficiently weak and the regime is sufficiently strong, making repression an extremely dangerous control device for a solidary group to invite.

A complementary and less risky error is the admission of a partisan group to access through an exaggerated estimate of their strength. In general, an error of repression is most likely when the authorities underestimate the strength and support of a solidary group; an error in granting access is most likely when the authorities overestimate the strength and support. It also follows that the less accurate the estimate of a solidary group's strength, the more likely it is to benefit by an access error. Or, put in other words, the more accurate the authorities are in their perception of a solidary group's strength, the less likely they are to make a social control error of this sort.

Similar considerations apply to social control errors in the use of constraints. Attempts to degrade and slander partisans can arouse sympathy and support for them among a wider group. If there is latent support, constraints may bring it into the open and thus strengthen the group. It may also succeed in scaring off some supporters, perhaps at the same time it helps the group grow. Attacks can do both simultaneously by polarizing the attitudes of potential followers.

A good illustration of the interplay between social control errors and the ebb and flow in the strength of a social movement is provided by an incident in the protest movement against American military actions in Vietnam. In October, 1965, a group of students staged a sit-in at a local Selective Service Board in Ann Arbor, Michigan, as part of a national protest against the war in Vietnam. This action and the generally strident tone of the protest helped to lend sustenance to administration charges that the protesters were an isolated fringe group without substantial wider sympathy in the community and nation. This impact was offset, however, by an error on the part of Selective Service officials. Several of the students were reclassified and this action rallied widespread support for the students on civil liberty grounds and brought the Selective Service System under a barrage of criticism. While the Selective Service System was only a subsidiary target for the protest movement, it was viewed as an instrument of the Vietnam policy and its self-created vulnerability proved a convenience to the protesters.

It is even possible to create increased pressure for change by persuasion errors involving what might be called a Frankenstein mechanism. Authorities may, in order to mobilize support for a policy, make strenuous efforts at persuading potential partisans through the mass media and in other ways. If such efforts are successful, the same officials may find themselves under fire from the very people most persuaded. For example, having made strenuous efforts to convince potential partisans of the righteousness of a war, the convinced partisans may use the administration's own arguments to press for dramatic military action which the administration is reluctant to undertake. "Overpersuasion" may generate pressure for more extreme action.

A Frankenstein mechanism may also work in the form of stimulating expectations which go unfulfilled. Broken promises fail to stimulate influence when they were regarded with cynicism in the first place. But making such promises more credible without fulfilling them makes them more likely to mobilize pressure for influence.

CONCLUSION

This book has argued that power and discontent can best be understood when viewed from the complementary perspectives of potential partisans and authorities. Much of the discussion has viewed things from the latter perspective but I would have to admit some justice to the charge that authorities have not fared well in this treatment. I have granted that one of their central functions is to produce binding decisions and that they spend most of their time doing this but the discussion here has focused much more on how they control potential partisans. Control has a pejorative ring, even when it is benevolently motivated, and authorities surely appear in a better light when we examine how they solve problems.

The emphasis on control comes from the focus in this book on decisions involving conflicts of interests and values. The other kinds of decisions, those involving collective interests and shared values, exist and are certainly worthy of discussion. If authorities are treated primarily as "controllers" here, they are certainly given their due as "leaders" elsewhere.

Sometimes authorities refuse to act as controllers and unobligingly contradict the central argument in this book. Nothing in the preceding pages would lead us to expect federal officials to push actively for "maximum participation of the poor" in the poverty program. If the analysis here is correct, it makes no sense that an alienated group which is not actively engaged in influence should be mobilized by a major target of its potential influence. It was not hard to anticipate that such alienated groups would begin to put pressure on urban political machines and that the influential leaders of such machines would, in turn, direct pressure at Washington. For poverty officials to urge the participation of the poor in their program can only be regarded as asking for trouble and, yet, such trouble was sought in this case.

Such anomalies exist and they put a different slant on the sources of social change. Some men in positions of authority have their own concerns about injustice and the adequacy of social institutions. When authorities begin identifying with alienated groups and their causes, presumably changes can come without influence "from below." Until that day, a little influence helps.

References

Almond, Gabriel A. and Verba, Sidney. *The Civic Culture.* Boston: Little, Brown & Co., 1965.

Bachrach, Peter and Baratz, Morton S. "Two Faces of Power," *American Political Science Review,* Vol. 56 (December, 1962), pp. 947-52.

Banfield, Edward. *Political Influence.* New York: The Free Press, 1961.

Bentley, Arthur F. *The Process of Government.* Chicago: University of Chicago Press, 1908.

Blau, Peter M. *Exchange and Power in Social Life.* New York: John Wiley & Sons, Inc., 1964.

Bottomore, T. B. and Rubel, Maximilien (eds.). *Karl Marx: Selected Writings in Sociology and Social Philosophy.* London: Watts and Co., 1956.

Burnham, James. *The Managerial Revolution.* New York: G. P. Putnam's Sons, 1941.

Campbell, Angus; Gurin, Gerald; and Miller, Warren E. *The Voter Decides.* Evanston, Ill.: Row, Peterson, 1954.

Campbell, Angus; Converse, Philip E.; Miller, Warren E.; and Stokes, Donald E. *The American Voter.* New York: John Wiley & Sons, Inc., 1960.

Campbell, Angus; Converse, Philip E.; Miller, Warren E.; and Stokes, Donald E. *Elections and the Political Order.* New York: John Wiley & Sons, Inc., 1966.

Carey, Alex. "The Hawthorne Studies: A Radical Criticism," *American Sociological Review,* Vol. 32 (June, 1967), pp. 403-16.

Cartwright, Dorwin. "A Field Theoretical Conception of Power," *Studies in Social Power.* (ed. Dorwin Cartwright), pp. 183-220. Ann Arbor, Mich.: Institute for Social Research, University of Michigan, 1959.

Cartwright, Dorwin (ed.). *Studies in Social Power.* Ann Arbor, Mich.: Institute for Social Research, University of Michigan, 1959.

Cartwright, Dorwin. "Influence, Leadership, Control," in *Handbook of Organizations.* (ed. James G. March), pp. 1-47. Chicago: Rand McNally, 1965.

Churchill, Winston. *The Second World War,* Vol. 4. New York: Bantam Books, Inc., 1962.

Coch, Lester and French, John R. P., Jr. "Overcoming Resistance to Change," in Harold Proshansky and Bernard Seidenberg, *Basic Studies in Social Psychology.* New York: Holt, Rinehart & Winston, Inc., 1965.

Coleman, James S. "Comment on 'On the Concept of Influence,' " *Public Opinion Quarterly,* Vol. 27 (Spring, 1963), pp. 63-82.

Dahl, Robert A. "The Concept of Power," *Behavioral Science,* Vol. 2 (July, 1957), pp. 201-18.

Dahl, Robert A. "A Critique of the Ruling Elite Model," *American Political Science Review,* Vol. 52 (June, 1958), pp. 463-69.

Dahl, Robert A. *Who Governs?* New Haven, Conn.: Yale University Press, 1961.

Dahl, Robert A. *Political Oppositions in Western Democracies.* New Haven, Conn.: Yale University Press, 1966.

Dahrendorf, Ralf. *Class and Class Conflict in Industrial Society.* Stanford, Calif.: Stanford University Press, 1959.

D'Antonio, William V. and Ehrlich, Howard J. (eds.). *Power and Democracy in America.* Notre Dame, Ind.: University of Notre Dame Press, 1961.

Deutsch, Karl. *The Nerves of Government.* New York: The Free Press, 1966.

Downs, Anthony. *An Economic Theory of Democracy.* New York: Harper & Row, 1957.

Easton, David. *The Political System.* New York: Alfred A. Knopf, Inc., 1953.

Easton, David. *A Systems Analysis of Political Life.* New York: John Wiley & Sons, Inc., 1965.

Egan, Conrad E. "Relationships between Community Power Structure Research and Community Organization," unpublished paper. April, 1967.

Emerson, Richard M. "Power-Dependence Relations," *American Sociological Review,* Vol. 27 (February, 1962), pp. 31-41.

Etzioni, Amitai. *A Comparative Analysis of Complex Organizations.* New York: The Free Press, 1961.

Fisher, Roger. "Fractionating Conflict," in *International Conflict and Behavioral Science* (ed. Roger Fisher), pp. 91-109. New York: Basic Books, Inc., Publishers, 1964.

Frank, Jerome D. "Experimental Studies of Personal Pressure and Resistance," *Journal of General Psychology,* Vol. 30 (1944), pp. 23-64.

French, John R. P., Jr., and Raven, Bertram. "The Bases of Social Power," in *Studies in Social Power* (ed. Dorwin Cartwright), pp. 150-67. Ann Arbor, Mich.: Institute for Social Research, University of Michigan, 1959.

Gamson, William A. "Community Issues and Their Outcome," in *Applied Sociology* (eds. Alvin W. Gouldner and S. M. Miller), pp. 350-57. New York: The Free Press, 1965.

Gamson, William A. "Rancorous Conflict in Community Politics," *American Sociological Review,* Vol. 31 (February, 1966), pp. 71-81 (a).

Gamson, William A. "Reputation and Resources in Community Politics," *American Journal of Sociology,* Vol. 72 (September, 1966), pp. 121-31 (b).

Gamson, Zelda F. "Social Control and Modification," Ph.D. Dissertation, Harvard University, 1964.

Gamson, Zelda F. "Utilitarian and Normative Orientations toward Education," *Sociology of Education,* Vol. 39 (Winter, 1966), pp. 46-73.

Geiger, Theodor. *Die Klassengesellschaft im Schmelztiegel.* Cologne and Hagen, 1949.

Gilman, G. "An Inquiry into the Nature and Use of Authority," in *Organization Theory in Industrial Practice* (ed. Mason Haire), pp. 105-42. New York: John Wiley & Sons, Inc.

Ginsberg, Morris. *Sociology.* Oxford: Oxford University Press, 1953.

Goffman, Erving. "On Cooling the Mark Out: Some Aspects of Adaptation to Failure," in Warren G. Bennis, *et al., Interpersonal Dynamics.* Homewood, Ill.: Dorsey Press, 1964, pp. 417-30.

Goldhamer, Herbert and Shils, Edward A. "Types of Power and Status," *American Journal of Sociology,* Vol. 45 (September, 1939), pp. 171-82.

Green, Arnold L. "The Ideology of Anti-Fluoridation Leaders," *Journal of Social Issues,* Vol. 17 (1961), pp. 13-25.

Guilford, J. P. *Psychometric Methods.* New York: McGraw-Hill Book, Inc., 1954.

Harsanyi, John C. "Measurement of Social Power, Opportunity Costs, and the Theory of Two-Person Bargaining Games," *Behavioral Science,* Vol. 7 (January, 1962), pp. 67-80.

Hawley, Amos H. "Community Power and Urban Renewal Success," *American Journal of Sociology,* Vol. 68 (January, 1963), pp. 422-31.

Homans, George C. *Social Behavior: Its Elementary Forms.* New York: Harcourt, Brace & World, Inc., 1961.

Hunter, Floyd. *Community Power Structure.* Chapel Hill, N.C.: University of North Carolina Press, 1953.

Janowitz, Morris. *The Professional Soldier.* New York: The Free Press, 1960.

Janowitz, Morris and Marvick, Dwaine. "Competitive Pressure and Democratic Consent," in Heinz Eulau, Samuel J. Eldersveld, and Morris Janowitz, *Political Behavior,* pp. 275-85. New York: The Free Press, 1956.

Jennings, M. Kent. *Community Influentials.* New York: The Free Press, 1964.

Kaufman, Herbert. "The Mystery of Power," *Public Administration Review,* Vol. 14 (Summer, 1954), pp. 205-12.

Kelman, Herbert C. "Processes of Opinion Change," *Public Opinion Quarterly,* Vol. 25 (Spring, 1961), pp. 57-78.

Key, V. O., Jr., *Politics, Parties, and Pressure Groups.* 3d ed. New York: Thomas Y. Crowell Co., 1952.

Kornhauser, William. *The Politics of Mass Society.* New York: The Free Press, 1959.

Lane, Robert E. *Political Life.* New York: The Free Press, 1959.

Lane, Robert E. *Political Ideology.* New York: The Free Press, 1962.

Lasswell, Harold D. *Psychopathology and Politics.* Chicago: University of Chicago Press, 1930.

Lasswell, Harold D. *Politics: Who Gets What, When, How.* New York: McGraw-Hill Book Co., 1936.

Lasswell, Harold D. and Kaplan, Abraham. *Power and Society.* New Haven, Conn.: Yale University Press, 1950.

Latham, Earl. *The Group Basis of Politics.* Ithaca, N.Y.: Cornell University Press, 1952.

Leeds, Ruth. "The Absorption of Protest," in William W. Cooper, Harold J. Leavitt, and Maynard W. Shelly, II, *New Perspectives in Organization Research,* pp. 115-35. New York: John Wiley & Sons, Inc., 1964.

Lerner, Daniel. *The Passing of Traditional Society.* New York: The Free Press, 1958.

Lieberman, Bernhardt. "*i*-Trust," Research Memorandum, S. P. 105. New York: Department of Psychology, State University at Stony Brook, 1963.

Lipset, Seymour Martin. *Political Man.* Garden City, N.Y.: Doubleday & Co., Inc., 1960.

Lowi, Theodore. "The Public Philosophy: Interest-Group Liberalism," *American Political Science Review,* Vol. 61 (March, 1967), pp. 5-24.

MacRae, Duncan and Price, Hugh D. "Scale Positions and 'Power' in the Senate," *Behavioral Science,* Vol. 4 (July, 1959), pp. 212-18.

Martin, Roscoe C. *et al. Decisions in Syracuse.* Garden City, N.Y.: Doubleday & Co., Inc., 1965.

Marx, Karl. *Selected Writings in Sociology and Social Philosophy* (eds. T. B. Bottomore and Maximilien Rubel). London: Watts and Company, 1956.

Milgram, Stanley. "Behavioral Study of Obedience," *Journal of Abnormal and Social Psychology,* Vol. 67 (1963), pp. 371-78.

Milgram, Stanley. "Group Pressure and Action against a Person," *Journal of Abnormal and Social Psychology,* Vol. 69 (1964), pp. 137-43.

Milgram, Stanley. "Some Conditions of Obedience and Disobedience to Authority," in *Current Studies in Social Psychology* (eds. Ivan D. Steiner and Martin Fishbein), pp. 243-62. New York: Holt, Rinehart, & Winston, Inc., 1965.

Mills, C. Wright. *The Power Elite.* New York: Oxford University Press, Inc., 1956.

Mitchell, William C. *The American Polity.* New York: The Free Press, 1962.

Modigliani, Andre. "Embarrassment and Social Influence," Ph.D. Dissertation, University of Michigan, 1966.

Neumann, Franz L. "Approaches to the Study of Political Power," *Political Science Quarterly,* Vol. 65 (1950), pp. 161-80.

Neumann, Franz L. *The Democratic and the Authoritarian State.* New York: The Free Press, 1957.

Neustadt, Richard E. *Presidential Power.* New York: John Wiley & Sons, Inc., 1962.

Oglesby, Carl. "March on Washington," Speech, November 27, 1965. (Reprinted in *Liberation,* 1966.)

Olson, Mancur, Jr. *The Logic of Collective Action.* Cambridge, Mass.: Harvard University Press, 1965.

Orne, Martin T. "On the Social Psychology of the Psychological Experiment," *American Psychologist,* Vol. 17 (1962), pp. 776-83.

Orne, Martin T. and Evans, Frederick J. "Social Control in the Psychological Experiment," *Journal of Personality and Social Psychology,* Vol. 1 (1965), pp. 189-200.

Parsons, Talcott. *The Structure of Social Action.* New York: McGraw-Hill Book Co., 1937.

Parsons, Talcott. " 'Voting' and the Equilibrium of the American Political System," in Eugene Burdick and Arthur J. Brodbeck, *American Voting Behavior.* New York: The Free Press, 1959.

Parsons, Talcott. *Structure and Process in Modern Societies.* New York: The Free Press, 1960.

Parsons, Talcott; Shils, Edward; Naegele, Kaspar D.; and Pitts, Jesse R. *Theories of Society.* New York: The Free Press, 1961.

Parsons, Talcott. "On the Concept of Influence," *Public Opinion Quarterly,* Vol. 27 (Spring, 1963), pp. 37-62.

Parsons, Talcott. "Some Reflections on the Place of Force in Social Process," in *Internal War* (ed. Harry Eckstein), pp. 33-70. New York: The Free Press, 1964.

Pepitone, Albert and Wallace, W. "Experimental Studies on the Dynamics of Hostility." Paper read at Pennsylvania Psychological Association Meetings, 1955. [Described in Albert Pepitone, "Attributions of Causality, Social Attitudes, and Cognitive Matching Processes," in *Person Perception and Interpersonal Behavior* (eds.) Renato Tagiuri and Luigi Petrullo), pp. 258-76. Stanford, Calif.: Stanford University Press, 1958.]

Pilisuk, Marc and Hayden, Thomas. "Is There a Military Industrial Complex Which Prevents Peace?" *Journal of Social Issues,* Vol. 21 (July, 1965), pp. 67-117.

Polsby, Nelson W. *Community Power and Political Theory*. New Haven, Conn.: Yale University Press, 1963.

Presthus, Robert. *Men at the Top*. New York: Oxford University Press, Inc., 1964.

Roethlisberger, F. J. and Dickson, W. J. *Management and the Worker*. Cambridge, Mass.: Harvard University Press, 1939.

Rosenau, James N. *Public Opinion and Foreign Policy*. New York: Random House, Inc., 1961.

Rosenberg, M. and Pearlin, L. I. "Power Orientations in the Mental Hospital," *Human Relations* (1962), pp. 335-50.

Rummel, Rudolph J. "The Dimensions of Conflict Behavior within and between Nations," *General Systems Yearbook*, Vol. 8 (1963), pp. 1-50.

Russell, Bertrand. *Power: A New Social Analysis*. London: George Allen and Unwin, Ltd., 1938.

Schattschneider, E. E. *The Semi-Sovereign People*. New York: Holt, Rinehart, & Winston, Inc., 1960.

Schelling, Thomas C. *The Strategy of Conflict*. Cambridge, Mass.: Harvard University Press, 1960.

Schlesinger, Arthur M., Jr. *A Thousand Days*. Boston: Houghton Mifflin Co., 1965.

Schramm, Wilbur. *Mass Communications*. Urbana, Ill.: University of Illinois Press, 1963.

Schumpeter, Joseph A. *Capitalism, Socialism, and Democracy*. New York: Harper & Bros., 1947.

Selznick, Philip. *TVA and the Grass Roots*. Berkeley, Calif.: University of California Press, 1953.

Simmel, Georg. *The Sociology of Georg Simmel* (ed. Kurt H. Wolff). New York: The Free Press, 1950.

Simon, Herbert A. *Models of Man*. New York: John Wiley & Sons, Inc., 1957.

Smelser, Neil J. *Theory of Collective Behavior*. New York: The Free Press, 1963.

Sykes, Gresham M. *The Society of Captives*. Princeton, N.J.: Princeton University Press, 1958.

Tanter, Raymond. "Dimensions of Conflict Behavior within Nations,

1955-60: Turmoil and Internal War," *Papers,* Vol. III, Peace Research Society, Philadelphia: University of Pennsylvania, Department of Regional Science, 1965.

Thibaut, John W. and Kelley, Harold H. *The Social Psychology of Groups.* New York: John Wiley & Sons, Inc., 1959.

Truman, David B. *The Governmental Process.* New York: Alfred A. Knopf, Inc., 1953.

Verba, Sidney. *Small Groups and Political Behavior.* Princeton, N.J.: Princeton University Press, 1961.

Weber, Max. *The Theory of Social and Economic Organization.* Oxford: Oxford University Press, 1947.

Wolfinger, Raymond E. "Reputation and Reality in the Study of 'Community Power,'" *American Sociological Review,* Vol. 25 (October, 1960), pp. 636-44.

Wolfinger, Raymond E. "A Plea for a Decent Burial," *American Sociological Review,* Vol. 27 (December, 1962), pp. 841-47.

Index